volume 3   20 Presentations for Winter

the complete guide to
Godly Play

Jerome W. Berryman

An imaginative method for presenting scripture stories to children

The scripture quotations used in this work are from the *New Revised Standard Version of the Bible.* © 1989 by the Division of Christian Education of the National Council of Churches of Christ in the USA. Used by permission.

ISBN 978-1-8891-0897-1

TABLE OF CONTENTS

INTRODUCTION

Welcome to *The Complete Guide to Godly Play, Volume 3.* In this volume, we gather together the presentations that form the suggested cycle of lessons for Winter. *Volume 1* of the series, *How to Lead Godly Play Lessons*, provides an in-depth overview of the process and methods of Godly Play. Below, you'll find only quick reminder notes. Please refer to *Volume 1* for an in-depth presentation.

Following this Introduction, you'll find all the information you need to present the lessons of Winter to the children in your Godly Play room. We hope the simple format will enable all teachers, whether new or experienced, to find the information they need to enter fully into the most rewarding play we share: Godly Play.

WHAT IS GODLY PLAY?

Godly Play is what Jerome Berryman calls his interpretation of Montessori religious education. It is an imaginative approach to working with children, an approach that supports, challenges, nourishes and guides their spiritual quest. It is more akin to spiritual direction than to what we generally think of as religious education.

Godly Play assumes that children have some experience of the mystery of the presence of God in their lives, but that they lack the language, permission and understanding to express and enjoy that in our culture. In Godly Play, we enter into parables, silence, sacred stories and sacred liturgy in order to discover God, ourselves, one another and the world around us.

In Godly Play, we prepare a special environment for children to work with adult guides. Two teachers guide the session, making time for the children:
• to enter the space and be greeted
• to get ready for the presentation
• to enter into a presentation based on a parable, sacred story or liturgical action
• to respond to the presentation through shared wondering
• to respond to the presentation (or other significant spiritual issue) with their own work, either expressive art or with the lesson materials
• to prepare and share a feast
• to say goodbye and leave the space

To help understand what Godly Play *is*, we can also take a look at what Godly Play is *not*. First, Godly Play is *not* a complete children's program. Christmas pageants, vacation Bible school, children's choirs, children's and youth groups, parent-child retreats, picnics, service opportunities and other components of a full and vibrant children's ministry are all important and are not in competition with Godly Play. What Godly Play contributes to the glorious mix of activities is the heart of the matter, the art of knowing and knowing how to use the language of the Christian people to make meaning about life and death.

Godly Play is different from many other approaches to children's work with scripture. One popular approach is having fun with scripture. That's an approach we might find in many church school pageants, vacation Bible schools or other such suggested children's activities.

Having superficial fun with scripture is fine, but children also need deeply *respectful* experiences with scripture if they are to fully enter into its power. If we leave out the heart of the matter, we risk trivializing the Christian way of life. We also miss the profound fun of existential discovery, a kind of "fun" that keeps us truly alive!

HOW DO YOU DO GODLY PLAY?

When doing Godly Play, *be patient*. With time, your own teaching style, informed by the practices of Godly Play, will emerge. Even if you use another curriculum for church school, you can begin to incorporate aspects of Godly Play into your practice —beginning with elements as simple as the greeting and goodbye.

Pay careful attention to the environment you provide for children. The Godly Play environment is an "open" environment in the sense that children may make genuine choices regarding both the materials they use and the process by which they work toward shared goals. The Godly Play environment is a "boundaried" environment in the sense that children are protected and guided to make constructive choices.

As teachers, we set nurturing boundaries for the Godly Play environment by managing *time, space* and *relationships* in a clear and firm way. The setting needs such limits to be the kind of safe place in which a creative encounter with God can flourish. Let's explore each of these in greater depth.

HOW TO MANAGE TIME

AN IDEAL SESSION

In its research setting, a full Godly Play session takes about two hours. An ideal session has four parts, each part echoing the way most Christians organize their worship together.

OPENING: ENTERING THE SPACE AND BUILDING THE CIRCLE

The storyteller sits in the circle, waiting for the children to enter. The door person helps children and parents separate outside the room, and helps the children slow down as they enter the room. The storyteller helps each child sit in a specific place in the circle, and greets each child warmly by name.

The storyteller, by modeling and direct instruction, helps the children get ready for the day's presentation.

HEARING THE WORD OF GOD: PRESENTATION AND RESPONSE

The storyteller first invites a child to move the hand of the Church "clock" wall hanging to the next block of color. The storyteller then presents the day's lesson. At the presentation's end, the storyteller invites the children to wonder together about the lesson. The storyteller then goes around the circle asking each child to choose work for the day. If necessary, the door person helps children get out their work, either storytelling materials or art supplies. As the children work, some might remain with the storyteller who presents another lesson to them. This smaller group is made up of those who aren't able to choose work on their own yet.

SHARING THE FEAST: PREPARING THE FEAST AND SHARING IT IN HOLY LEISURE

The door person helps three children set out the feast—such as juice, fruit or cookies—for the children to share. Children take turns saying prayers, whether silently or aloud, until the last prayer is said by the storyteller. The children and storyteller share the feast, then clean things up and put the waste in the trash.

DISMISSAL: SAYING GOODBYE AND LEAVING THE SPACE

The children get ready to say goodbye. The door person calls each child by name to say goodbye to the storyteller. The storyteller holds out hands, letting the child make the decision to hug, hold hands or not touch at all. The storyteller says goodbye and reflects on the pleasure of having the child in this community.

In the research setting, the opening, presentation of the lesson and wondering aloud together about the lesson might take about half an hour. The children's response to the lesson through art, retelling and other work might take about an hour. The preparation for the feast, the feast and saying goodbye might take another half an hour.

IF YOU ONLY HAVE THE FAMOUS FORTY-FIVE MINUTE HOUR

You may have a limited time for your sessions—as little as forty-five minutes instead of two hours. With a forty-five-minute session, you have several choices.

FOCUS ON THE FEAST

Sometimes children take especially long to get ready. If you need a full fifteen minutes to build the circle, you can move directly to the feast, leaving time for a leisurely goodbye. You will not shortchange the children. The quality of time and relationships that the children experience within the space *is* the most important lesson presented in a session of Godly Play.

FOCUS ON THE WORD

Most often, you will have time for a single presentation, including time for the children and you to respond to the lesson by wondering together. Finish with the feast and then the goodbye ritual. Because the children will have no time to make a work response, we suggest that every three or four sessions, you omit any presentation and focus on the work instead (see directly below).

FOCUS ON THE WORK

If you usually must pass from the presentation directly to the feast, then every three or four sessions, substitute a work session for a presentation. First build the circle. Then, without making a presentation, help children choose their work for the day. Allow enough time at the end of the session to share the feast and say goodbye.

PLANNING THE CHURCH YEAR

We've simplified annual planning by presenting the lessons in their suggested seasonal order of presentation.

In Fall, an opening session on the Church year is followed by Old Testament stories, from creation through the prophets. In Winter, we present the season of Advent and the Feasts of Christmas and Epiphany, followed by the parables. In spring, we present the faces of Christ during Lent, followed by Easter presentations of the resurrection, the Eucharist and the early Church.

Not all groups will—or should!—follow this suggested order. Some possible exceptions:
- Groups with regularly scheduled short sessions will need to substitute work sessions for presentations every third or fourth Sunday.
- If the storyteller is not yet comfortable with a particular presentation, we recommend substituting a work session for that day's presentation.
- Within a work session, one child might request the repetition of an earlier presentation. Another child might ask a question that draws on an enrichment presentation; for example, "Why do we have crosses in church?" That's a "teachable moment" to bring out the object box of crosses.

HOW TO MANAGE SPACE

GETTING STARTED

We strongly recommend a thorough reading of *The Complete Guide to Godly Play, Volume 1: How to Lead Godly Play Lessons*.

To start, focus on the relationships and actions that are essential to Godly Play, rather than on the materials needed in a fully equipped Godly Place space. We know that not every parish can allocate generous funds for Christian education. We believe Godly Play is worth beginning with the simplest of resources. Without any materials at all, two teachers can make a Godly Play space that greets the children, shares a feast and blesses them goodbye each week.

When Jerome Berryman began his teaching, he used shelving made from boards and cinder blocks, and only one presentation material: figures for the parable of the Good Shepherd, cut from construction paper and placed in a shoe box he had spray-painted gold.

Over the year, Berryman filled the shelves with additional homemade lesson materials. When more time and money became available, he upgraded those materials to ones cut from foamcore. Now his research room is fully equipped with the full range of beautiful and lasting Godly Play materials: parable boxes, Noah's ark, a desert box filled with sand. All of these riches are wonderful gifts to the children who spend time there, but the *start* of a successful Godly Play environment is the nurturing of appropriate relationships in a safe space.

MATERIALS

MATERIALS FOR PRESENTATIONS

Each lesson details the materials needed in a section titled "Notes on the Materials." You can make materials yourself, or order beautifully crafted materials from:

Morehouse Education Resources
4775 Linglestown Rd.
Harrisburg, PA 17112
(800) 242-1918
fax: (717) 541-8136
www.morehouseeducation.org

Here is a list of all suggested materials for the presentations of the Winter quarter:

- *throughout the year (for all or many of the lessons)*
  — circle of the Church year (wall hanging)
  — set of crèche figures
  — cloths in liturgical colors (white, purple, red, green)
  — figure of the Risen Christ
  — juice, fruit and/or cookies
  — matzo

- *Enrichment Lesson: Holy Family*
  — Holy Family figures

— figure of the Risen Christ
— cloths in liturgical colors (white, purple, red, green)

- *Lesson 1: Advent I*
  — Advent cards
  — 4 Advent candles
  — matches in a metal container
  — candle snuffer
  — model of Bethlehem

- *Lesson 2: Advent II*
  — Advent cards
  — 4 Advent candles
  — matches in a metal container
  — candle snuffer
  — model of Bethlehem
  — Holy Family figures

- *Lesson 3: Advent III*
  — Advent cards
  — 4 Advent candles
  — matches in a metal container
  — candle snuffer
  — model of Bethlehem
  — Holy Family figures

- *Lesson 4: Advent IV*
  — Advent cards
  — 4 Advent candles
  — matches in a metal container
  — candle snuffer
  — model of Bethlehem
  — Holy Family figures
  — Christ Candle

- *Enrichment: A Children's Liturgy for Christmas Eve*
  — parish crèche figures (stable, Mary, Joseph, animals, etc.)

- *Enrichment: The Mystery of Christmas*
  — pictures, labels and texts mounted on foamcore or wood

- *Lesson 5: Epiphany*
  — Advent cards

— 4 Advent candles
— matches in a metal container
— candle snuffer
— model of Bethlehem
— Holy Family figures
— Christ Candle
— frankincense, myrrh, gold-covered coins
— tweezers

- *Lesson 6: Holy Baptism*
  — bowl
  — pitcher of water
  — dove
  — container of fragrant oil
  — metal box of matches
  — Christ Candle
  — snuffer
  — baby doll, wrapped in white blanket or gown
  — brass bowl of sand
  — basket of candles, with drip guards

- *Lesson 7: Parable of the Good Shepherd*
  — gold parable box with green dot
  — 12 brown felt strips
  — 3 black felt shapes
  — blue felt shape
  — 5 sheep
  — Good Shepherd
  — ordinary shepherd
  — wolf

- *Lesson 8: Parable of the Good Samaritan*
  — gold parable box with dark brown dot
  — light brown felt road
  — 2 black felt pieces
  — 2 city shapes
  — 6 people (1 injured person, 2 thieves, 1 priest, 1 Levite, 1 Samaritan),
  — 1 "covering piece" (picture of Samaritan helping injured person)

- *Lesson 9: Parable of the Great Pearl*
  — gold parable box with white dot
  — 5 brown rectangular places
  — 2 figures (merchant and seller)
  — merchant's possessions (money, chest, bed, candle, vase, chair, footstool)

- *Lesson 10: Parable of the Sower*
  — gold parable box with light brown dot
  — gold box of birds
  — 3 earth images (rocky soil, thorns, good earth)
  — 3 bags of grain
  — sower

- *Lesson 11: Parable of the Leaven*
  — gold parable box with tan dot
  — woman figure
  — table
  — box containing loaf of bread (1 flat piece and 1 risen piece) and 3 bowls of flour
  — box with triangular gold leave

- *Lesson 12: Parable of the Mustard Seed*
  — gold parable box with yellow dot
  — green felt shrub (or tree)
  — gold box with birds and nests
  — figure of a person

- *Enrichment Lesson: Parable of Parables*
  — set of nesting boxes in assorted colors

- *Enrichment Lesson: Parable of the Deep Well*
  — plain parable box
  — well
  — container of golden threads
  — bucket

- *Enrichment Lesson: Parable Synthesis 1—All the Parables*
  — 40 gold parable cards
  — 15 gold "I Am" cards
  — Bible

- *Enrichment Lesson: Parable Synthesis 2—The "I Am" Statements*
  — 40 gold parable cards
  — 15 gold "I Am" cards
  — box for sorting
  — box with context cards

- *Enrichment Lesson: Parable Synthesis 3—The Parable Games*
  — 40 gold parable cards
  — 23 gold parable game cards

MATERIALS FOR CHILDREN'S WORK

Gather art supplies that the children can use to make their responses. These materials are kept on the art shelves. We suggest:

- paper
- painting trays
- watercolor paints and brushes
- drawing boards
- crayons, pencils and markers
- boards for modeling clay
- clay rolled into small balls in airtight containers

MATERIALS FOR THE FEAST

- napkins
- serving basket
- cups
- tray
- pitcher

MATERIALS FOR CLEANUP

Gather cleaning materials that the children can use to clean up after their work and use to care for their environment. We suggest:

- paper towels
- feather duster
- brush and dustpan
- cleaning cloths
- spray bottles with water
- trash can with liner

HOW TO ARRANGE MATERIALS

The materials are arranged to communicate visually and silently the language system of the Christian faith: our sacred stories, parables and our liturgical actions. Main presentations are generally kept on the top shelves.

Enrichment presentations are generally kept on the second shelves. Bottom shelves are kept free for supplemental materials, such as books, maps or other resources. Separate shelves hold supplies for art, cleanup and the feast. A shelf for children's work in progress is also very important.

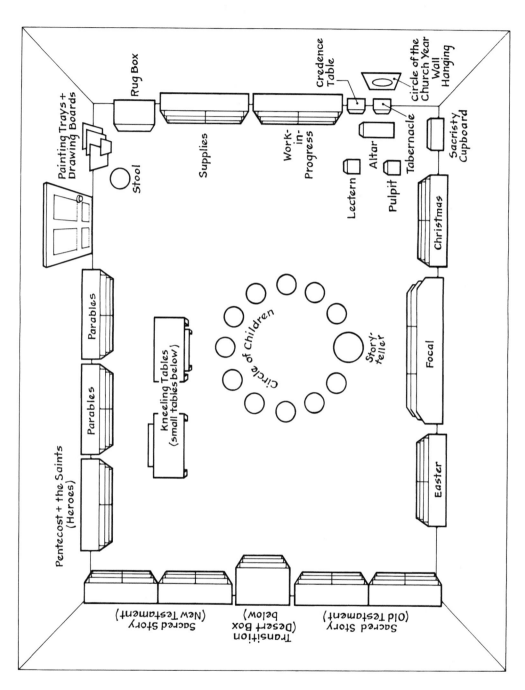

THE GODLY PLAY ROOM

HOW TO MANAGE RELATIONSHIPS

THE TWO TEACHING ROLES:
DOOR PERSON AND STORYTELLER

Each teaching role fosters respect for the children and the Godly Play space. For example, parents are left at the threshold of the Godly Play space and teachers remain at the children's eye level. Both practices keep the room child-centered, instead of adult-centered.

Similarly when the storyteller presents a lesson, he or she keeps eye focus on the materials of the lesson—not the children. Instead of being encouraged to respond to a teacher, the children are invited, by the storyteller's eyes, to enter the story.

In a typical Sunday morning session, only two adults will be present in the Godly Play space: the door person and the storyteller. These are their respective tasks during a typical session:

DOOR PERSON

Check the shelves, especially the supply shelves and art shelves.

Get out the roll book, review notes and get ready to greet the children and parents.

Slow down the children coming into the room. You may need to take and put aside toys, books and other distracting objects. Help them to get ready. Take the roll or have the older children check themselves in.

Close the door when it is time. Be ready to work with latecomers and children who come to you from the circle.

Avoid casual eye contact with the story-teller to help prevent the adults in the room from turning the children into objects, talking down to them or manipulating them.

STORYTELLER

Check the material to be presented that day.

Get seated on the floor in the circle and prepare to greet the children.

Guide the children to places in the circle where they will best be able to attend to the lesson. Visit quietly until it is time to begin and all are ready.

Present the lesson. Model how to "enter" the material.

Draw the children into the lesson by your introduction. Bring your gaze down to focus on the material when you begin the actual lesson. Look up when the wondering begins.

DOOR PERSON

When the children choose their work, they may need help setting up artwork and getting materials from the shelves for work on a lesson, either alone or in a group.

Stay in your chair unless children need your help. Do not intrude on the community of children. Stay at the eye level of the children whenever possible, as if there is a glass ceiling in the room at the level of the taller children.

Help the children put their work away, and also help the children who are getting ready to lay out the feast.

Sit quietly in your chair. Be sure that the trash can has a liner in it.

Greet the parents and begin to call the names of the children who are ready and whose parents are there.

If a child starts for the door without saying goodbye to the storyteller, remind him or her to return to the storyteller to say goodbye.

STORYTELLER

After the lesson and wondering, go around the circle, dismissing each child to begin his or her work, one at a time. Each child chooses what to do. Go quickly around the circle the first time, returning to the children who did not decide. Go around the circle for decisions until only a few are left. These may be new or for some other reason cannot make a choice. Present a lesson to these children.

Remain seated in the circle unless children need help with the lessons they have gotten out. You may need to help with art materials. Keep yourself at the children's eye level as you help.

When it is time for the feast, go to the light switch and turn it off. Ask the children to put their work away and come back to the circle for the feast. Turn the light back on. Go to the circle to anchor it as the children finish their work and return.

Ask for prayers, but do not pressure. After the feast, show the children how to put their things away in the trash.

Help the children get ready to have their names called.

As the children's names are called, they come to you. Hold out your hands. Children can take your hands, give a hug or keep their distance, as they like. Tell them quietly and privately how glad you were to see them and what good work they did today. Invite them to come back when they can.

DOOR PERSON

Remember to give back anything that may have been taken at the beginning of class.

When the children are gone, check and clean the art and supply shelves.

Sit quietly and contemplate the session as a whole.

Evaluate, make notes and discuss the session with your coteacher.

STORYTELLER

Take time to enjoy saying goodbye, with all the warmth of a blessing for each child.

When all are gone, check the material shelves and clean.

Sit quietly and contemplate the session as a whole.

Evaluate the session, record your notes and discuss the session with your coteacher.

HOW OTHERS CAN HELP

Other adults who want to support the work of a Godly Play space can contribute by:
- taking turns providing festive and healthy food for the children to share during their feasts
- keeping the art and supply shelves replenished with fresh materials
- using their creative skills to make materials for Godly Play presentations

HOW TO RESPOND EFFECTIVELY TO DISRUPTIONS IN THE CIRCLE

You always want to model the behavior you expect in the circle: focused on the lesson and respectful of everyone in the circle. If a disruption occurs, you deal with that disruption in such a way that you still show continual respect for everyone in the circle—including the child who is having trouble that day. You also still maintain as much focus on the lesson as you can, returning to complete focus on the lesson as quickly as possible.

Therefore, as you consider responses, remember to keep a neutral tone in your voice. Remember, too, that our goal is to help the child move himself or herself toward more appropriate behavior. At the first level of interruption, you might simply raise your eyes from the material. You look up, but not directly at the child, while saying, "We need to get ready again. Watch. This is how we get ready." Model the way to get ready and begin again the presentation where you left off.

If the interruption continues or increases, address the child directly. "No, that's not fair. Look at all these children who are listening. They are ready. You need to be ready, too. Let's try again. Good. That's the way."

If the interruption still continues or increases, ask the child to sit by the door person. Don't think of this as a punishment or as an exclusion from the story: some children *want* to sit by the door person for their own reasons. Continue to keep a neutral tone of voice as you say, "I think you need to sit by Ann. *(Use the door person's name.)* You can see and hear from there. The lesson is still for you."

The goal is for the child to take himself or herself to the door. If the child is having trouble, or says, "No!", you can say, "May I help you?" Only if necessary do you gently pick up the child or, in some similar way, help him or her go to the door person.

HOW TO SUPPORT THE CHILDREN'S WORK

Show respect for the children's work in two key ways: through the structure of the classroom in which the children work and through the language you use—and do *not* use—in talking about their work. Let's explore each of these.

CLASSROOM STRUCTURE

A Godly Play classroom is structured to support children's work in four ways:

- First, it makes *materials* inviting and available by keeping the room open, clean and well-organized. A useful phrase for a Godly Play room is, "This material is for you. You can touch this and work with this when you want to. If you haven't had the lesson, ask one of the other children or the storyteller to show it to you." Children walking into a Godly Play classroom take delight at all the fascinating materials calling out to them. These materials say, "This room is for you."
- Second, it encourages responsible *stewardship* of the shared materials by helping children learn to take care of the room themselves. When something spills, we could quickly wipe it up ourselves, of course. Instead, by helping children learn to take care of their own spills, we communicate to them the respect we have for their own problem-solving capabilities. At the end of work time, each child learns to put away materials carefully. In fact, some children may want to choose cleaning work—dusting or watering plants—for their entire response time.
- Third, it provides a respectful *place* for children's work by reserving space in the room for ongoing or finished projects. When a child is still working on a project at the end of work time, reassure him or her by saying, "This project will be here for you next week. You can take as many weeks as you need to finish it. We never lose work in a Godly Play room." Sometimes children want to give a finished piece of work to the room. Sometimes children want to take either finished or unfinished work home. These choices are theirs to make, and ours to respect.
- Fourth, it sets a leisurely *pace* that allows children to engage deeply in their chosen responses. This is why it's better to do no more than build the circle, share a feast and lovingly say goodbye when we are pressed for time rather than rush through a story and time of art response. When we tell a story, we want to allow enough time

for leisurely wondering together. When we provide work time, we want to allow enough time for children to become deeply engaged in their work. In their wondering or their work, children may be dealing with deep issues—issues that matter as much as life and death. Provide them a nourishing space filled with safe *time* for this deep work.

USING LANGUAGE

You can also support children with the language you use:

- Choose *"open" responses*. We choose "open" responses when we simply describe what we see, rather than evaluate the children or their work. Open responses invite children's interaction, but respect children's choices to simply keep working in silence, too. *Examples:*
  — Hm. Lots of red.
  — This is big work. The paint goes all the way from here to there.
  — This clay looks so smooth and thin now.
- Avoid *evaluative responses*. Evaluative responses shift the child's focus from his or her work to your praise. In a Godly Play classroom, we want to allow children the freedom to work on what matters most to them, not for the reward of our praise. *Examples to avoid:*
  — You're a wonderful painter.
  — This is a great picture.
  — I'm so pleased with what you did.
- Choose *empowering responses*, which emphasize each child's ability to make choices, solve problems and articulate needs. In a Godly Play classroom, a frequently heard phrase is, "That's the way. You can do this." We encourage children to choose their own work, get the materials out carefully and clean up their work areas when they are done. When a child spills something, respond with, "That's no problem. Do you know where the cleanup supplies are kept?" If a child needs help, show where the supplies are kept or how to wring out a sponge. When helping, the aim is to restore ownership of the problem or situation to the child as soon as possible.
- Stay alert to the children's *needs* during work and cleanup time. The door person's role is especially important as children get out and put away their work. By staying alert to the children's choices in the circle, the door person can know when to help a new child learn the routine for using clay, when a child might need help moving the desert box or when a child might need support in putting material away or cleaning up after painting.

MORE INFORMATION ON GODLY PLAY

The Complete Guide to Godly Play, Volumes 1-8 by Jerome Berryman are available from Morehouse Education Resources. *Volume 1: How to Lead Godly Play Lessons* is the essential handbook for using Godly Play in church school or a wide variety of alternative settings. *Volumes 2-4* present complete presentations for Fall, Winter and Spring. *Volumes 6-8* contain a series of enrichment lessons to be integrated with *Volumes 2, 3, and 4. Volume 5* includes the wisdom of Godly Play trainers.

The *Godly Play Foundation* is the nonprofit organization that sponsors ongoing research, training, development of materials, accreditation programs, the development of a theology of childhood, and supports high-quality Godly Play practice around the world.

The *Godly Play Foundation* is an ecumenical and parish-based organization with centers of excellence in this country and around the world. For locations of these centers please visit our Web site at *www.godlyplay.org*

The *Foundation* maintains a schedule of training and speaking events related to Godly Play, and a list of trainers available throughout this and other countries for help in establishing Godly Play programs. For more information, contact:

Godly Play Foundation
Physical address: 1551 10 Ave. E, Seattle, WA 98102
Mailing address: P.O. Box 23320, Seattle, WA 98102
Phone: 206-619-3145
www.godlyplay.org
center@godlyplay.org

Although you can make your own materials, Morehouse Education Resources now supplies the beautiful and lasting materials approved by the *Godly Play Foundation* especially for use in a Godly Play classroom. For more information or to place an order, contact:

Morehouse Education Resources
4775 Linglestown Road
Harrisburg, PA 17112
1-800-242-1918
fax: 1-717-541-8136
www.morehouseeducation.org

ENRICHMENT LESSON
THE HOLY FAMILY

LESSON NOTES

FOCUS: AXIS OF THE CHRISTIAN LANGUAGE SYSTEM: THE BIRTH, LIFE, DEATH AND RESURRECTION OF JESUS CHRIST

● LITURGICAL ACTION

● ENRICHMENT PRESENTATION

THE MATERIAL

● LOCATION: FOCAL SHELVES

● PIECES: HOLY FAMILY AND FIGURE OF THE RISEN CHRIST

● UNDERLAY: NONE

BACKGROUND

We first present this lesson at the beginning of the church-school year. We repeat the lesson whenever we change the liturgical colors in the room to reflect the changes in the liturgical season—purple or blue for Advent, white for Christmas, green for Epiphany and so on. On those occasions, one purpose of the lesson is simple: we take the Holy Family off the shelf, change the colored cloth on the shelf to a new one, then replace the figures on the new cloth.

However, the Holy Family holds deep significance for our work throughout the year. That is why it sits right in the center of the focal shelves in the room—right behind the storyteller—every week of the year. That is why we draw attention to it in this presentation to the children every time we change liturgical colors. The Holy Family is the *matrix*—the Latin word for womb—out of which new life comes. This story is the story of the re-creation of the universe. Christ's incarnation changes everything. Most especially, it changes the way we understand ourselves, each other, the Creator and the created world around us.

We find existential meaning in our lives, in the places into which we are born, through the network of these relationships. The "answer" to life is not a propositional statement or verbal key. Instead of an answer, we find a "home," every day, in the midst of these relationships of love and creating.

The axis of life in the Christian tradition is birth-death-rebirth. The children begin to perceive this axis through the naming of the Holy Family, and through the careful, respectful moving of the figures. We do not talk about this meaning, but wait for the children themselves to discover it. We, like the Holy Family, are invited to be cocreators in the biological, psychological, social and spiritual spheres of life.

NOTES ON THE MATERIAL

The material is a Nativity set with these figures: Mary, Joseph, the Christ Child (removable, with outstretched arms), a shepherd, one or more sheep, a donkey, a cow and the three kings, together with a figure of the Risen Christ with outstretched arms. Any size will do, but 4"-6" figures work well for young children. Children can easily handle these small figures, and they won't take up as much room on the shelf. Behind the Holy Family, place the Risen Christ with outstretched arms.

If possible, find figures that are not too detailed or realistic, so that children can supply details through their imaginations. More figures or more complex figures will not work as well as the simple set described above. Don't include a stable; it distracts from the Holy Family.

In an ideal setup, the focal shelves are the shelving unit directly opposite the door through which the children enter. The Holy Family sits in the center of the top shelf of the focal shelves. To the right of the Holy Family, also on the top shelf, is the green circle with the figure of the Good Shepherd and his sheep, from the material for World Communion (see *The Complete Guide to Godly Play, Volume 4)*. To the left of the Holy Family stands a tall white candle called the Light (or the Christ Candle).

On the shelves below the Good Shepherd are the remaining materials for the World Communion lesson. Below the Light on the second shelf are the remaining materials for the lesson about Holy Baptism (see *The Complete Guide to Godly Play, Volume 3*). Below the Holy Family on the second shelf is a tray that contains the colored cloths of the liturgical year and a circular tray lined with white felt. You will use these two trays whenever you change liturgical colors during the year. On the bottom shelf is the material for the Circle of the Church Year.

SPECIAL NOTES

Classroom Management: Children can use the felt-lined tray when they work with the Holy Family, but most children will prefer to keep the figures on the top focus shelf as they move them around.

We suggest you tell this story three times in the Winter season. On the first Sunday of Advent, use the story to change the cloth underneath the Holy Family from green to purple or blue. On Christmas, Epiphany or the feast of the Baptism of Our Lord, use the story to change the cloth underneath the Holy Family from purple or blue to white. On the first Sunday after these feasts (Ordinary Time or Epiphany season), use the story to change the cloth from white to green.

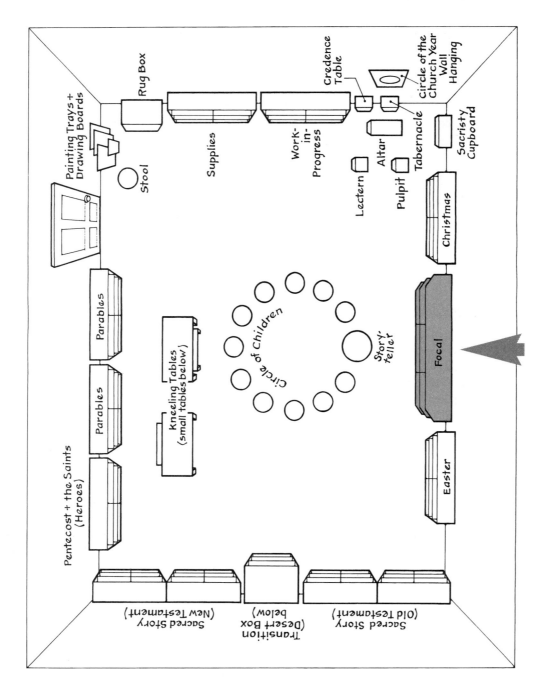

WHERE TO FIND MATERIALS

MOVEMENTS

The storyteller sits in front of the focal shelves. In the center of the top shelf is the Holy Family, which rests on a cloth colored to match the liturgical time of year—red for Pentecost, white for Easter, and so on. Behind the Holy Family, there is a picture or carving of the Risen Christ.

Tell this story whenever you want to change the color of the cloth underneath the Holy Family, the focal point of the room throughout the year. For this lesson, the Holy Family is already resting on a green cloth. In this telling, you will change the cloth to purple or blue, to match the liturgical color used in your church for Advent.

When the children are settled in the circle, you begin. Go to the rug box and get a rug. Return to the circle and roll it out. Turn and take out the round tray for the Holy Family from the lower shelves behind you. It is large enough to hold all the figures of the Holy Family. The bottom of the tray is covered with white felt.

Move to the side so the children can see the Holy Family on the shelf behind you. Turn toward the shelf and open your hands to show what you are going to talk about. Wait until you are present to the story yourself before beginning.

Pick up the Christ Child from the manger and hold it in the palm of your hand for all the children to see.

WORDS

➤ This is the Holy Family. Sometimes when you see something like this, it is not for children to touch. It might break easily, so you need to ask if you can touch it or work with it. This Holy Family is for you. It is for you to touch and work with. You don't need to ask to work with it.

➤ This is the Christ Child. He is holding out his arms to give you a hug.

MOVEMENTS	WORDS

THE HOLY FAMILY

Put the manger on the white circle tray in front of you. Replace the Christ Child in the manger.

Hold Mary in the palm of your hand as well, showing her to the children. Then place her behind the manger, looking across it to the children.

⟹ Here is the mother Mary.

Hold Joseph in the palm of your hand and then place him next to Mary.

⟹ Here is the father, Joseph.

Hold out the donkey and then place it beside Mary.

⟹ Here is the donkey that Mary rode when she and Joseph went to Bethlehem to be counted by the Roman soldiers. Mary was about to have a baby, so it was hard for her to walk. Sometimes she rode on the donkey. It is also hard to ride on a donkey when you are about to have a baby, so she got down again and walked.

Hold out the cow and then place it beside Joseph.

⟹ Here is the cow that was in the stable when the baby was born. He was surprised to find a baby in the feed box, the manger, where he usually found his breakfast.

Hold out the shepherd and sheep and then place them facing toward the Christ Child on the other side of the manger from Mary and Joseph.

⟹ Here is the shepherd who saw the great light in the sky at night. There were more shepherds than this, but we will put down one to remind us. Here are some of the sheep. There were more, but these will do to help us remember.

MOVEMENTS	WORDS
	When they saw the light in the darkness, they were afraid. I would be, too. Then they heard singing. That scared them, too, until they heard the words. The angels sang that they came to bring peace on earth and good will to all people. "Run. Hurry. Go to Bethlehem. Something has happened there that changes everything!"
Hold out the three Magi and place them as you speak.	Here are the three kings, the wise men. They were so wise that people thought they were magic. In their language they were called the Magi, and that word is the word from which we get our word *magic.* They knew so much that people thought they were magic. And of all the things they knew, they knew the most about the stars.
	One day they saw the wild star. The Magi knew where all the stars were supposed to be in the sky, but this star moved. This star was not on their maps of the sky. So when it moved, they were curious, and followed it. It led them to the stable where the Christ Child was born.
	The wise men brought with them gifts for the Christ Child: gold, frankincense and myrrh.
Pick up the Christ Child from the manger. Hold out the Christ Child to the children and continue holding him as you speak.	Here is the little baby reaching out to give you a hug. He grew up to be a man and died on the cross. That is very sad, but it is also wonderful, in an Easter kind of way.
Move the Christ Child slowly and with dignity to the figure of the Risen Christ. Superimpose the baby with outstretched arms on the Risen Christ's outstretched arms.	Now he can reach out and give the whole world a hug. He is not just back then, in this place or that place. He is everywhere, and in every time.

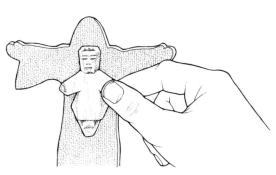

THE CHRIST CHILD AND THE RISEN CHRIST

MOVEMENTS

Return the Christ Child to the manger. Sit back and quietly take in the whole scene. Be present to its meaning.

Roll up the green underlay from the top shelf of the focal shelves. Place it on the tray of liturgical cloths on the middle shelf of the focal shelves. From this same tray, take out the purple or blue cloth and roll it out on the top shelf.

You now begin to replace the Holy Family, one by one, without hurrying, naming each one as you slowly and with care put them back on the purple cloth. (Whether placing the figures on the white tray, or returning them to the focal shelf, use the layout illustrated on p. 24.)

Pause and then begin the wondering with the children.

Sit back as the wondering draws to a close. Enjoy what has been said and done. Then begin to go around the circle to help the children choose their work, one at a time.

WORDS

Here is the Baby Jesus.
Here is the Mother Mary.
Here is the Father Joseph.
Here is the donkey that Mary rode on.
Here is the cow that was so surprised in the morning.
Here is one of the shepherds and a few of the sheep.
Here are the wise men, the three kings, the Magi.

This is the Holy Family, and you can work with these figures any time you wish. In our classroom, they are for you.

Now I wonder what part of the Holy Family you like best?

I wonder what part of the Holy Family is the most important part?

I wonder if you have ever seen any of the Holy Family in our church?

I wonder if there is any of the Holy Family we can leave out and still have all we need?

Now it is time to get out our work. What work would you like to get out today? You may work with the Holy Family, or you may make something about them. Maybe you have something that you are already working on. There may be another material you would like to work with. There is so much. While I am going around the circle, think about what you are going to work with.

ADVENT I

LESSON NOTES

FOCUS: THE PROPHETS

● *LITURGICAL ACTION*

● *CORE PRESENTATION*

THE MATERIAL

● *LOCATION: FOCAL SHELVES AND CHRISTMAS SHELVES*

● *PIECES: ADVENT CARDS ON A RACK OR TRAY; 4 ADVENT CANDLES IN A BOX, MATCHES IN A METAL CONTAINER AND A CANDLE SNUFFER, ALL ON A TRAY; PURPLE OR BLUE CLOTH OR FELT; MODEL OF BETHLEHEM; OPTIONAL: CANDLE HOLDERS*

● *UNDERLAY: PURPLE (OR BLUE) AND WHITE*

BACKGROUND

This lesson, together with the next three lessons, helps the children to anticipate the mystery of Christmas. We move toward Bethlehem and arrive at the birth of Jesus and the lighting of the Christ Candle in the church.

Churches often have customs that preclude doing a single lesson about Advent on each of the Sundays of the season. For example, the whole congregation might use the first Sunday to make Advent wreaths together, or use the fourth Sunday to hold a Christmas party for the children. In such situations, group the lessons as seems best to you, presenting two or even three Advent cards on one Sunday. Remember, too, to start the first Advent session together by telling the story of the Holy Family (pp. 20-26), in order to change the liturgical color from green to purple (or blue).

NOTES ON THE MATERIAL

Find the materials for this presentation on the Christmas shelves and the focal shelves. The Christmas shelves are to the left of the focal shelves. The model of Bethlehem stands to the far left on the top shelf of the Christmas shelves. In the middle of the top shelf you'll find the tray or rack of Advent cards. The box of candles, container of matches and candle snuffer are on a tray at the left end of the second shelf (below the model of Bethlehem).

A special stand or carrier rack for the Advent cards makes them visible to a child scanning the room. This stand for the cards should also hold the rolled-up underlay. If you do not use this stand, put the rolled-up underlay and cards in a tray. You may want to line the tray with purple or blue cloth or felt.

There are five cards or wooden plaques, representing, in this order:
- the prophets
- the Holy Family
- the shepherds
- the Magi
- the birth of Jesus

These cards or plaques are laid on a strip of cloth divided into five equal sections, one section for each of the four weeks of Advent, plus an additional section for the feast of Christmas. The first four sections of this cloth are purple or blue (for Advent); the fifth and final section is white (for Christmas). This cloth is the Advent underlay; roll up the underlay so that the white segment is hidden inside. (An illustration of the underlay, with all five cards or plaques and candles laid out in order, appears in Lesson 5, p. 68.)

Many churches use blue for their Advent color. In this presentation, we refer to the liturgical color purple, but use whatever color your church uses. Instead of referring to the royal color (purple), point out that blue is a good color for getting ready, because it is the color associated with Mary, Jesus' mother. Without the mother Mary, there would be no baby.

You also need a box to hold the four candles used in the lesson. In this presentation, we refer to one rose and three purple candles, but, again, follow the custom of your church. Use candles with wide bases for stability (e.g., votives or pillar candles), or, if you use tapers, also use candle holders. You also need a metal container for matches; look in an import store for beautiful and inexpensive metal containers. Though this container may tarnish quickly, some children may enjoy keeping it polished in the classroom! You will also need a candle snuffer. Keep these items (candles, matches and snuffer) on a tray lined with purple or blue cloth or felt.

Finally, you need a model of the city of Bethlehem, similar to that pictured on page 31. It is to be set in the middle of the circle of children to show that we are all on the way to Bethlehem, including the storyteller.

SPECIAL NOTES

Classroom Management: Working with fire during the work period is problematic. It means something different for different ages or for different children. Some children need more supervision than others. Sometimes children are more attracted to the fire than to the meaning of this lesson, so they need a lot of support and supervision to get past that. This attraction, however, is still a point of entry into the lesson, so don't worry too much about why they are interested. Only be aware that these are the very children that need the most supervision. One pragmatic way to address these issues is by making a rule for *everyone* that the storyteller always lights the candles.

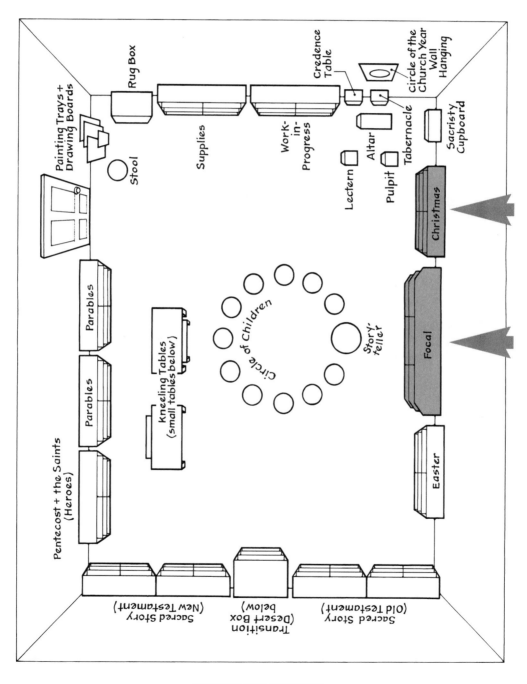

WHERE TO FIND MATERIALS

MOVEMENTS

When the children are ready, go to the Christmas shelves.

Bring the cards and underlay (on the rack or tray) to the circle and place them beside where you will be sitting. Then, in a separate trip, bring the tray holding the box of candles, container of matches and candle snuffer; again, set this beside where you will sit. Finally, in a third trip, bring the model of Bethlehem and set it in the middle of the circle. On each trip, walk carefully and handle the materials with respect. Be seated and wait until everyone is ready, then begin.

Start to roll out the underlay as you introduce the color of Advent, the season of getting ready. Only unroll as much underlay as is needed to hold the first Advent card.

Move your hand over the purple.

WORDS

Watch carefully where I go so you will always know where to find this lesson.

Everything is changed. It is now the time of the color purple.

Purple is the color of kings and queens. No one could wear purple in those days except royal people. Roman citizens could wear a little stripe of purple, but that was all. Purple is a serious color, and something serious is about to happen. A King is coming, but he is not the kind of king that people thought was coming. This King had no army, no great house, and no riches. This King was a baby who was born in a barn.

The King who was coming is still coming. This is full of mystery. You know, a mystery is hard to enter sometimes. That is why this time of Advent is so important. Sometimes people can walk right through a mystery and not even know it is there. This time of year you will see people hurrying in the malls buying things and doing this and that, but they will miss the Mystery. They don't know how to get ready or maybe they just forgot.

The Church learned a long time ago that people need a way to get ready to enter or even come close to a mystery like Christmas. The Church set aside four weeks to get ready. This is such a great Mystery that it takes that long to get ready. During this time, we are all on the way to Bethlehem. We are all making the

MOVEMENTS	WORDS
	journey. We are all getting ready to enter the Mystery of Christmas, so let's go with the prophets, the Holy Family, the shepherds, the angels, the Magi and all the rest to make the journey that was not just back then. It is also now.
Place the first Advent card in its section of the underlay. The first card shows one lit Advent candle and a prophetic hand pointing the way.	Prophets are people who come so close to God, and God comes so close to them, that they know what is most important.

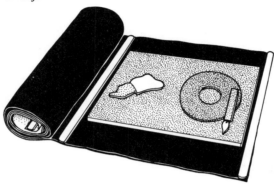

THE FIRST ADVENT CARD (STORYTELLER'S PERSPECTIVE)

Point to the model of Bethlehem that you put in the middle of the circle when the lesson began.	They pointed the way to Bethlehem. They didn't know exactly what was going to happen there, but they knew this was the place.

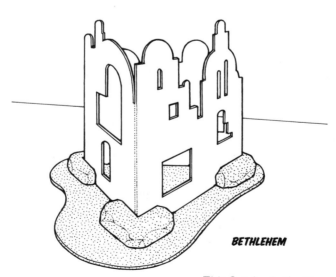

BETHLEHEM

This Sunday is the time we remember the prophets. Here is the hand of a prophet pointing the way to Bethlehem, showing us the way, too.

MOVEMENTS	WORDS
Point again. Be emphatic, bold, definite.	➠ Stop. Watch. Pay attention. Something incredible is going to happen in Bethlehem.
Place the first of the purple candles between you and the section of the underlay with the card on it. Pick up the container with the matches in it. Open the container, strike a match and light the candle.	➠ This is the light of the prophets. Let's enjoy the light.
Sit for a moment and genuinely enjoy the light of the prophets. You might even have the door person, with a nod from you, turn out the light, so the candlelight is more visible. Sometimes the candles burn down inside so that all the children see is the light glowing within the candle or the glow over the top of the candle. The storyteller looks down into the candle and sees the flame, but the children may not.	➠ Prophets are the people who know the most important things. They knew which way to go. They are the ones who showed us the way. Now we can go to Bethlehem, too.
If you turned off the light, have the door person turn it back on now. Pick up the candle snuffer.	➠ I want to show you something very strange and very important. Look.
	I want to show you what happens when the light is changed. Sometimes people don't pay attention to this. They miss this part.
	Look. Do you see how the flame is in just one place now? It is right here. When I change the light, it will no longer be in just one place. You can't see it after it spreads out all over the room, but it is there.
Snuff the candle. Hold the snuffer over the flame for it to fill with smoke. When you lift it, the smoke will rise and begin to spread out.	➠ Watch. Do you see it? It is no longer here in this one place. Now it is spreading out, getting thinner and thinner as it fills up the room with the light of the prophets. Anywhere you go in this room you will be close to the prophets.
	There may even be one sitting in this circle. Prophets can be boys, and prophets can be girls. They pay attention. They know things.

MOVEMENTS

Enjoy the moment and then begin to put the material back. There is no wondering at the end of this lesson. It is better to let the presence of the prophets rest in the room.

Carry Bethlehem back to its shelf first. Then put the card and the underlay back in their rack (or tray) and return the rack to its shelf. Put away the candle tray last, making certain the wax in the candle has had time to cool, so that it will not spill out into the cloth-lined tray. Be certain that the matches are secure in their container.

When everything is put away, come back to the circle and begin to help the children make their decisions about what work to get out next.

WORDS

Now watch carefully where I go with this material, so you will always know where to get it when you want to work with it.

LESSON 2
ADVENT II

LESSON NOTES

FOCUS: THE HOLY FAMILY

- LITURGICAL ACTION
- CORE PRESENTATION

THE MATERIAL

- LOCATION: FOCAL SHELVES AND CHRISTMAS SHELVES
- PIECES: ADVENT CARDS ON A RACK OR TRAY; 4 ADVENT CANDLES IN A BOX, MATCHES IN A METAL CONTAINER AND A CANDLE SNUFFER, ALL ON A TRAY; PURPLE OR BLUE CLOTH OR FELT; NATIVITY SET FIGURES OF MARY, JOSEPH AND THE DONKEY; MODEL OF BETHLEHEM; OPTIONAL: CANDLE HOLDERS
- UNDERLAY: PURPLE (OR BLUE) AND WHITE

BACKGROUND

This lesson helps children continue to prepare for the Mystery of Christmas. We move toward Bethlehem, guided by the pointing prophets, with the Holy Family, the shepherds and the Magi. We arrive at the birth of Jesus and the lighting of the Christ Candle in the church. This week's presentation focuses on the Holy Family.

You begin this week's lesson by presenting the first of the four Advent cards and telling about the prophets; see Lesson 1, pages 27-33 for the movements and words.

In this lesson, you then add the second Advent card and tell the story of the Holy Family.

NOTES ON THE MATERIAL

Your will find the material for this presentation on the Christmas shelves and the focal shelves. For a complete description of these materials, see the Notes on the Material in Lesson 1, page 27.

SPECIAL NOTES

Classroom Management: You'll find a useful tip about working with fire on page 28. Another issue that can arise with the Advent presentations is resistance on the part of older children to language about "getting ready to enter the Mystery." Supporting children as they struggle with their resistance is part of our art. These children do not yet know how the language of the Christian people works. There is little experience of this language in our culture, and certainly none in their formal schooling.

Don't give in to their honest—or sometimes not so honest—complaints about being bored or already having had this lesson. Sometimes children resist simply to be disruptive or even to avoid the discomfort of intimacy.

Affirm that being a part of the story is not easy. God never said it was easy. You never said it was easy. It is not easy like arithmetic. Arithmetic is a way of speaking that is always the same. $2+2=4$. In elementary arithmetic, this is always correct. $12-4=8$. Lovely. Arithmetic is comforting. It keeps things in order!

Religious language also gives order to our lives, as in going to church each Sunday, going to church for weddings and funerals, and by observing the seasons of the Church year. When it gives order, it also asks us to find what is new and different in the sameness. Religious language is generative language: it calls us to be who we are really supposed to be, creatures who create.

This lesson is different from math and science in another way. We are trying to enter into a mystery. We want to come as close to it as we can. You can't do that and at the same time stand back and measure it or analyze it. You can't add three mysteries to four mysteries to see what the sum of a mystery is. Each mystery enters into the sum of all mystery. The mystery of Christmas is more like a door to enter than a wall on which to write numbers or draw pictures.

What is important in this sort of language is finding your way into a meaning, a meaning that grows. In religious language there is always more. It is like a well that is never empty. You can become tired of such a challenge, but the language and its source is never exhausted nor emptied.

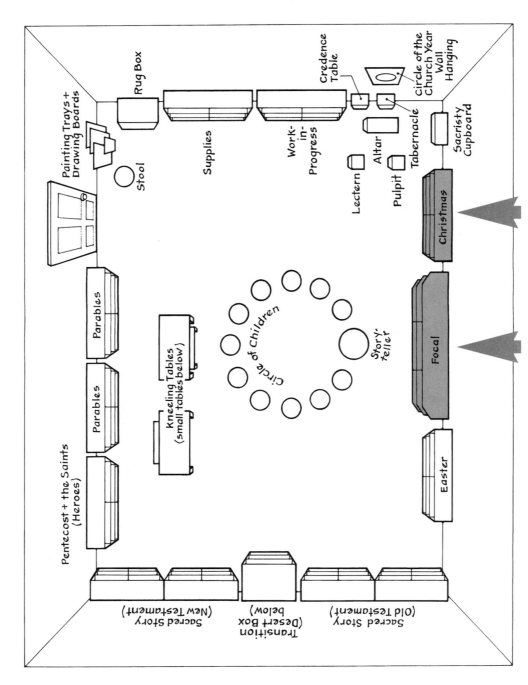

WHERE TO FIND MATERIALS

MOVEMENTS	WORDS
When the children are ready, go to the Christmas shelves and get the materials you need, as described in Lesson 1, Advent I (p. 30).	Watch carefully where I go so you will always know where to find this lesson.
Place the first Advent card and tell about the prophets. Do not minimize or rush that first story. End with the words: "Something incredible is going to happen in Bethlehem."	
Unroll the underlay to uncover the next section. Place the second Advent card to your left of the first card. The second card shows two candles lit and an image of Bethlehem.	This is the card of the Holy Family.
Point to the symbol of Bethlehem on the card.	Do you see Bethlehem on the card, and the road? The Holy Family is on the way to Bethlehem and we are going with them.

THE FIRST AND SECOND ADVENT CARDS (STORYTELLER'S PERSPECTIVE)

Turn around to the focal shelves behind you. Take Mary from the Holy Family on the center of the top shelf and place her on the card, close to you.	Here is the Mother Mary.
Next take the Joseph figure and place him on the card.	Here is the Father Joseph.
Place the donkey figure on the card, between Mary and Joseph.	Here is the donkey.

MOVEMENTS

WORDS

Mary was about to have a baby. It is very hard to walk when you are about to have a baby. Sometimes she could not take another step. Then she rode on the donkey.

It is also hard to ride on a donkey when you are about to have a baby. When she couldn't ride another step, she got down and walked. She rode and she walked.

They must have been the last people coming up the road to Bethlehem that night.

Sit back and enjoy how, in this second week of Advent, we are all on the way to the Mystery of Christmas. Then get out two candles and light them.

Here is the light of the prophets. Here is the light of the Mother Mary and the Father Joseph as they make their way to Bethlehem.

Let's enjoy the light.

The door person can turn out the classroom lights so the children can see the candles glow. Sit back and enjoy the light.

If you turned off the light, have the door person turn it back on now. Pick up the candle snuffer from the candle tray.

Now watch. I am going to change the light. Do you see how the light of the prophets is just in one place? I am going to change the light so that it can be in every place.

Snuff the first candle. Hold the snuffer over the flame for it to fill with smoke. When you lift it, the smoke will rise and begin to spread out. Then snuff the second candle in the same way.

Watch. Do you see how the light of the mother Mary and the father Joseph is just in this one place? I am going to change the light so that it can be in every place.

Do you see how the light is not gone? It is changed. It is not in one place. Now it is spreading out, getting thinner and thinner, to fill up the whole room. The room is filling up with the light of the prophets and with the light of the mother Mary and the father Joseph. Anywhere you go in this room you can come close to them today.

Enjoy the moment and then begin to put the lesson back. There is no wondering at the end of this lesson.

Now watch carefully where I go with this material, so you will always know where to get it when you want to work with it.

MOVEMENTS

WORDS

Carry Bethlehem back to its shelf first. Then put the card and the underlay back in their rack (or tray) and return the rack to its shelf. Return Mary, Joseph and the donkey to the focal shelves. Put away the candle tray last, making certain the wax in the candles has had time to cool, so that it will not spill out into the cloth-lined tray. Be certain that the matches are secure in their container.

When everything is put away, come back to the circle and begin to help the children make their decisions about what work to get out next.

LESSON 3
ADVENT III

LESSON NOTES
FOCUS: THE SHEPHERDS
- ● *LITURGICAL ACTION*
- ● *CORE PRESENTATION*

THE MATERIAL
- ● *LOCATION: FOCAL SHELVES AND CHRISTMAS SHELVES*
- ● *PIECES: ADVENT CARDS ON A RACK OR TRAY; FOUR ADVENT CANDLES IN A BOX, MATCHES IN A METAL CONTAINER AND A CANDLE SNUFFER, ALL ON A TRAY; PURPLE OR BLUE CLOTH OR FELT; NATIVITY SET FIGURES OF MARY, JOSEPH, DONKEY, SHEPHERD AND SHEEP); MODEL OF BETHLEHEM; OPTIONAL: CANDLE HOLDERS*
- ● *UNDERLAY: PURPLE (OR BLUE) AND WHITE*

BACKGROUND

This lesson helps children continue to prepare for the Mystery of Christmas. We move toward Bethlehem, guided by the pointing prophets, with the Holy Family, the shepherds and the Magi. We arrive at the birth of Jesus and the lighting of the Christ Candle in the church. This week's presentation focuses on the shepherds.

You begin this week's lesson by presenting the first and second of the four Advent cards and telling the stories found in Lesson 1 (pp. 27-33) and Lesson 2 (pp. 34-39).

In this lesson, you then add the third Advent card and tell the story of the shepherds.

NOTES ON THE MATERIAL

Your will find the material for this presentation on the Christmas shelves and the focal shelves. For a complete description of these materials, see the Notes on the Material in Lesson 1, page 27.

SPECIAL NOTES

Classroom Management: This is the third Advent presentation we offer. If next week your church will skip church school for either a party or pageant, you'll want to include Lesson 4 today, thus completing all four Advent cards and their stories in your presentation.

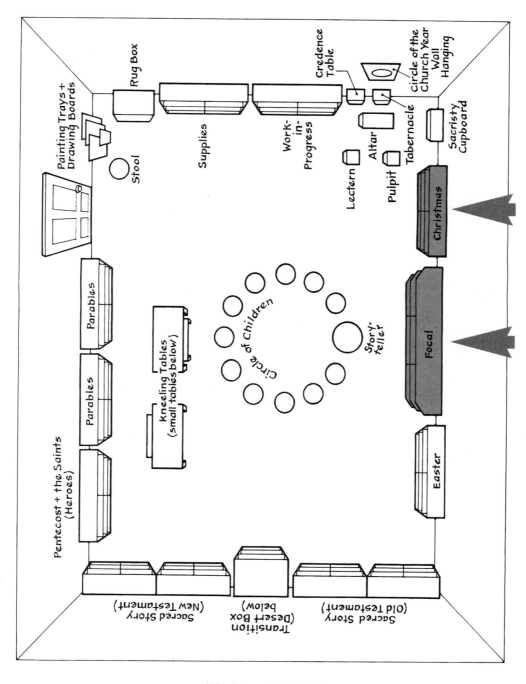

WHERE TO FIND MATERIALS

MOVEMENTS

When the children are ready, go to the Christmas shelves and get the materials you need, as described in Lesson 1 (p. 30) and listed at the beginning of this lesson.

Place the first Advent card and tell about the prophets (pp. 30-32). Do not minimize or rush the story. End with the words: "Something incredible is going to happen in Bethlehem."

Place the second Advent card and tell about the Holy Family (pp. 37-38). Do not minimize or rush this second story. End with the words: "They must have been the last people coming up the road to Bethlehem that night."

When you have finished, unroll the underlay to uncover the next section. Place the third Advent card to your left of the second card. The third card shows three lit candles and an image of a sheep.

WORDS

Watch carefully where I go so you will always know where to find this lesson.

This is the card of the shepherds.

THE FIRST, SECOND AND THIRD ADVENT CARDS (STORYTELLER'S PERSPECTIVE)

Turn around to the focal shelves behind you. Take the shepherd and the sheep and place them on the third Advent card, close to you.

On the third Sunday in Advent we remember the shepherds who were standing in the fields around Bethlehem keeping their sheep. They were trying to stay awake so the wolves could not come and get the sheep. Suddenly there was so much light in the sky that it hurt their eyes.

MOVEMENTS	WORDS
Pat your chest to make the sound of a heart beating.	They were afraid. Their hearts were beating so loudly. When they could hear something besides their own hearts, they thought they heard singing in the sky! That also scared them until they heard the words of the song. The angels were singing, "Don't be afraid." Angels often say that, because it is scary to have a messenger of God come to you.

The angels singing sounded something like this: "Don't be afraid. We bring you tidings of great joy. Peace on earth and good will to everyone. A Child is born. Go. Hurry. Run to Bethlehem to see the Child who will change everything." |
| *Place three candles, one by one, between you and the three cards on the underlay.* | Here is the candle of the prophets. This is the candle of the Holy Family. Here is the candle of the shepherds. |
| *Point to the third candle.* | Look—there is something different about this candle. It is the color of roses. This is to remind us of the great joy the angels sang of. It also helps us remember that even if it is very serious to get ready to come close to a great mystery like Christmas, you can't be serious all of the time as you get ready. This is the Sunday when it is time for a little celebration!

There is one more thing about the color of roses. It is also one of the colors for the mother Mary. We remember her again, for without the mother Mary, there would be no baby. |
Light the candles.	Let's enjoy the light.
Sit back and enjoy the light. The door person can turn out the classroom lights so the children can see the candles glow.	
If you turned off the light, have the door person turn it back on now. Take out the candle snuffer from the candle tray.	Now I am going to change the light. Do you see how the light of the prophets is just in one place? That is very helpful. That helps us see the light. Watch.
Snuff out the three candles slowly, as if doing it for the first time. Take time for the interpretation of what you are doing. Take time for the words.	Now it is changed, and the light that was in just one place is now spreading out. It gets more invisible as it spreads out. Soon it will fill up the whole room.

MOVEMENTS

WORDS

Here is the light of the Holy Family. It is easy to see when it is all gathered in one place. Now watch; I am going to change the light. Look. It too is spreading out. Do you see figures in the smoke? Watch how it changes. Look. It is spreading out and filling up the whole room. Just because it is hard to see doesn't mean that it isn't there.

And here is the light of the shepherds and the mother Mary again. I am going to change the light. Do you see how it is in one place? Now it can go be in every place. Look. It is filling up the room with the shepherds and mixing with the Holy Family and the prophets. Anywhere you go in the room today they will be there.

Enjoy the moment and then begin to put the lesson back. There is no wondering at the end of this lesson.

Now watch carefully where I go with this material, so you will always know where to get it when you want to work with it.

Carry Bethlehem back to its shelf first. Then put the cards and the underlay back in their rack (or tray) and return the rack to its shelf. Return the nativity figures to the focal shelves. Put away the candle tray last, making certain the wax in the candles has had time to cool, so that it will not spill out into the cloth-lined tray. Be certain that the matches are secured in their container.

When everything is put away, come back to the circle and begin to help the children make their decisions about what work to get out next.

LESSON 4
ADVENT IV

LESSON NOTES
FOCUS: THE WISE MEN AND CHRISTMAS
- LITURGICAL ACTION
- CORE PRESENTATION

THE MATERIAL
- LOCATION: FOCAL SHELVES AND CHRISTMAS SHELVES
- PIECES: ADVENT CARDS ON A RACK OR TRAY; 4 ADVENT CANDLES IN A BOX, MATCHES IN A METAL CONTAINER AND A CANDLE SNUFFER, ALL ON A TRAY; PURPLE OR BLUE CLOTH OR FELT; NATIVITY SET FIGURES OF MARY, JOSEPH, DONKEY, SHEPHERD, SHEEP, WISE MEN, CHRIST CHILD, MANGER); MODEL OF BETHLEHEM; OPTIONAL: CANDLE HOLDERS
- UNDERLAY: PURPLE (OR BLUE) AND WHITE

BACKGROUND

This lesson helps children continue to prepare for the Mystery of Christmas. We move toward Bethlehem, guided by the pointing prophets, with the Holy Family, the shepherds and the Magi. We arrive at the birth of Jesus and the lighting of the Christ Candle in the church. This week's presentation focuses on the wise men and the celebration of Christmas.

You begin this week's lesson by presenting the first, second and third of the four Advent cards and telling the stories found in Lesson 1 (pp. 27-33), Lesson 2 (pp. 34-39) and Lesson 3 (pp. 40-44).

You then add:
- the fourth and final Advent card, telling the story of the wise men, contained in this lesson
- the Christmas card, telling the story of Jesus' birth, also contained in this lesson

NOTES ON THE MATERIAL

Your will find the material for this presentation on the Christmas shelves and the focal shelves. For a complete description of these materials, see the Notes on the Material in Lesson 1, page 27.

In addition to the materials described in Lesson 1, you will also need the Christ Candle, which sits to the left of the Holy Family on the top shelf of the focal shelves. This candle will be used after Christmas, too, when you tell the story of Baptism.

SPECIAL NOTES

Classroom Management: Usually children do not come to church school on Christmas Eve or Christmas Day. Therefore, we suggest you complete the children's preparation for the Mystery of Christmas by laying out the fifth card as well, the white Christmas card that will be placed on the white section of the purple and white (or blue and white) underlay.

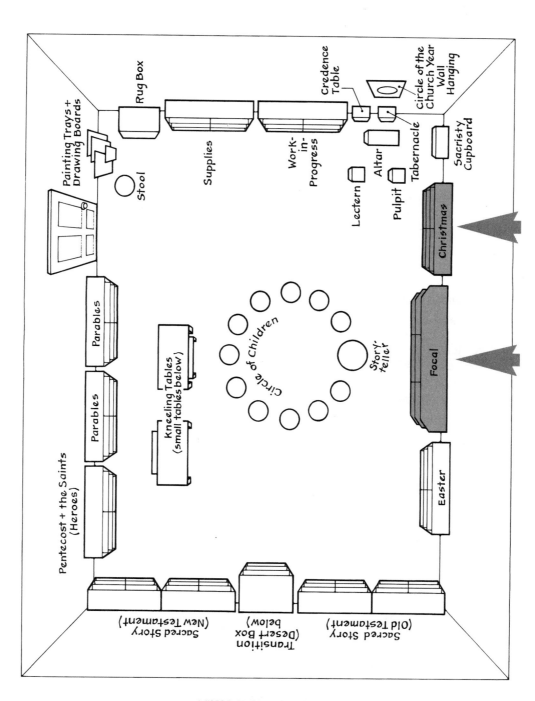

WHERE TO FIND MATERIALS

MOVEMENTS

When the children are ready, go to the Christmas shelves and get the materials you need, as described in Lesson 1, Advent 1 (p. 30).

Place the first Advent card and tell about the prophets (pp. 30-32). Do not minimize or rush the story. End with the words: "Something incredible is going to happen in Bethlehem."

Place the second Advent card and tell about the Holy Family (pp. 37-38). Do not minimize or rush the story. End with the words: "They must have been the last people coming up the road to Bethlehem that night."

Place the third Advent card and tell about the shepherds (pp. 42-43). Do not minimize or rush the story. End with the words: "Run to Bethlehem to see the child who will change everything."

When you have finished, unroll the underlay to uncover the next section. Place the fourth Advent card to your left of the third card. The fourth card shows four candles lit and an image of three crowns, which also look like the three gifts.

WORDS

⏩ Watch carefully where I go so you will always know where to find this lesson.

⏩ This is the card of the wise men.

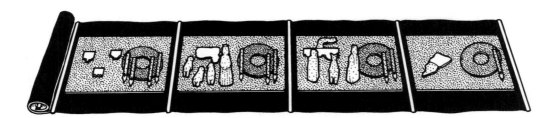

THE FOUR ADVENT CARDS (STORYTELLER'S PERSPECTIVE)

MOVEMENTS	WORDS
Turn around to the focal shelves behind you. Take the wise men, place them on the fourth Advent card, close to you.	On the fourth Sunday in Advent we remember the three kings, the Magi, the wise men. They came from far in the East, and they were so wise that people thought they were magic. In fact we get our word, "magic," from the name they were called in their own language, "the Magi."
As you talk about the stars, look up and then at your hands as if they were a book and point into the sky to note the proper places of the stars.	Of all the things they knew, they knew the most about the stars. They knew where each star was supposed to be at each time of the year, so they could tell people when it was time to plant their crops, or take a trip on the ocean in a boat, or cross the high mountain passes when the snow wasn't too deep.
	Suddenly they saw the wild star. It was not on any of their star maps. It went where it wanted to go. It did not stay put. They decided to follow the wild star to see where it was going and what it wanted to show them.
	They followed the star all the way to Bethlehem, but they came from so far away that they got there after the baby was born. They are always late, it seems. Every year they are late. They usually don't arrive until January 6th, but we remember them anyway, because, like us, they too are on the way to Bethlehem.
Place four candles, one by one, between you and the underlay with the cards on it.	Here is the candle of the prophets. This is the candle of the Holy Family. Here is the candle of the shepherds. Here is the candle of the wise men.
Now light the candles.	Let's enjoy the light.
Sit back and enjoy the light. Then, instead of snuffing the candles, unroll the fifth and final segment of the underlay, which is white.	Look! When you come to the mystery of Christmas, everything changes. It becomes the color of pure celebration.
Move your hand over the white.	This is when the baby is born, the one we have been waiting for.
Lay down the white card for Christmas. Then slowly turn around to the focal shelves behind you. Take the baby in the manger and place him in the middle of the white card.	Here is the Christ Child, the mystery of Christmas. This is amazing, but of all the creatures there that night, perhaps the most amazed was the old cow.

MOVEMENTS

Slowly turn back to the focal shelves and pick up the cow. Turn back and place the cow by the manger.

Sit back for a moment. Look at everything that has been placed before the children. Look around at the children. Touch the materials of the lesson laid before you all. Then say:

Wait. The children will probably discover quickly that the white card needs a candle, too. This is the Christ Candle that sits to the left of the Holy Family material, on the top shelf of the focal shelves.

Place this candle in the line with the four Advent candles.

Light the Christ Candle. Sit back and enjoy the light. The door person can turn out the classroom lights so the children can see the candles' glow.

WORDS

When the old cow came up to the feed box in the morning to eat some straw it found a baby lying in the manger. Someone had put a soft cover over the straw. The manger had become a bed. All the old cow could do was look and look at the baby with its big brown eyes.

Wait. Something is missing! I wonder what it could be?

This is the Christ candle. Now, let's enjoy its light, too.

LIGHTING THE CHRIST CANDLE

MOVEMENTS

If you turned off the light, have the door person turn it back on now. Take out the candle snuffer from the candle tray.

Snuff out all the candles slowly.

Enjoy the moment and then begin to put the lesson back. There is no wondering at the end of this lesson.

Carry Bethlehem back to its shelf first. Then put the cards and the underlay back in their rack (or tray) and return the rack to its shelf. Return the nativity figures to the focal shelves. Put away the candle tray last, making certain the wax in the candle has had time to cool, so that it will not spill out into the cloth-lined tray. Be certain that the matches are secured in their container.

When everything is put away, come back to the circle and begin to help the children make their decisions about what work to get out next.

WORDS

Now watch. I am going to change the light.

Now I am going to change the light of the Christ candle. Look. It too is spreading out to fill up the room. As it spreads out, it gets thinner and thinner until you can't see it at all. That doesn't mean that it's gone. It only means that you can't see it. You can still feel the Christmas light. It is filling up the room with the prophets, the Holy Family, the shepherds and the three kings. Anywhere you go, you can come close to them.

Now watch carefully where I go with this material, so you will always know where to get it when you want to work with it.

ENRICHMENT LESSON

A CHILDREN'S LITURGY FOR CHRISTMAS EVE

LESSON NOTES

FOCUS: THE NATIVITY STORY AS LITURGY

- LITURGICAL ACTION
- ENRICHMENT PRESENTATION

THE MATERIAL

- LOCATION: WHEREVER YOUR PARISH DISPLAYS ITS PARISH CRECHE FIGURES
- PIECES: PARISH CRECHE FIGURES (STABLE, MARY, JOSEPH, ANIMALS, ETC.)
- UNDERLAY: NONE

BACKGROUND

This presentation can be used as a sermon before or during the main Christmas Eve liturgy, or as a brief, separate children's service. A storyteller tells the story, which is punctuated by several familiar Christmas hymns. During these hymns, fourth- and fifth-grade children bring the crèche figures from the back of the church to the chancel. At the end of the story, all the children come forward—with their parents, if necessary—to place stars around and in the crèche as everyone sings "Silent Night." In the main liturgy, as people come forward for Holy Communion, they will pass by this star-decorated scene.

NOTES ON THE MATERIAL

Most parishes have a large-sized crèche that is visible to the congregation. This material can be used in this liturgy, or groups of children and adults can make the crèche figures from papier-mâché or other material suitable for large-scale modeling.

SPECIAL NOTES

Tip: Be sure to plan well ahead of time if you would like your church to include this liturgy in its Christmas celebration. Be willing to adapt the story, music or actions to the needs of your congregation.

MOVEMENTS

Stand where you can be heard by the entire congregation, perhaps in the pulpit or at the lectern from which the lessons are read. A crib should already be placed in the chancel. Older children, who will bring the figures forward, should be standing with these figures at the back of the church as you begin.

The older children now bring forward the donkey, the cow and the sheep as all the people sing verse one of "O Little Town of Bethlehem."

After the hymn, resume telling the story.

The older children now bring forward Mary and Joseph as all the people sing verse one of the hymn "Once in Royal David's City."

After the hymn, resume telling the story.

WORDS

This night is like no other night. It is a time to dream and sing our way to Bethlehem. The children will show us how to go.

The little town we seek sits in the hill country some ten miles south of Jerusalem. For thousands of years the houses have gathered there on the hilltop like a family breaking bread. "Bethlehem" *means* "House of Bread."

In the center of the village is a small inn. On this night it is overflowing with people seeking sleep and a place to eat. Be-hind the inn is a dark stable. A gray donkey chews his barley and broken straw while a weary cow leans and rests after the day's plowing in the valley. A sheep nearby is nearly asleep.

All is still and quiet in the little town.

As night gathers, the last two travelers come slowly up the road. Look, there is a young woman about to be a mother. She is walking with her husband. They are Joseph and Mary from Nazareth! They have walked for six days to come to this city where King David was born, so long ago.

They have come, like so many others, because the Roman emperor wants to count each one, so he can take their money as a tax.

But it is late, and Mary is so weary. Where will they sleep? There is no room in the inn. They decide to sleep with the animals.

Stars brighten slowly in the sky. All creation holds its breath. Suddenly, from the stable, comes the cry of a newborn child! Mary gently wraps the baby in a blanket and lays him in the feed box that his father has filled with straw.

MOVEMENTS

WORDS

One or some of the older girls now bring forward the baby Jesus as all the people sing verse one of the hymn "Away in a Manger."

After the hymn, resume telling the story.

In the hills outside Bethlehem, shepherds watch their shadowy sheep. All at once, the dark is lost in light, and in the midst of the light is something even brighter: the faces of angels.

The fearful shepherds then hear music in the sky, and a voice says clearly, "Do not be afraid. Listen, I bring you news of great joy, a joy to be shared by all people. Today in the City of David a Savior is born! He is Christ, the Lord."

Then more angels appear, a whole heavenly host of them, praising God and singing: "Glory to God in the highest, and on earth peace, good will to all people, everywhere."

The shepherds run with joy across the fields to Bethlehem to the barn behind the inn. There they find the Holy Family and creep forward, overwhelmed with mystery, to find Nativity itself in the center of all that love.

The older children now bring forward the shepherds and the angel as all the people sing verse one of the hymn "While Shepherds Watched."

After the hymn, resume telling the story.

Three camels plod up the road to Bethlehem. They have come from the East, far beyond the Arabian Desert, perhaps from as far as the Caspian Sea. The camels carry three kings, the wise ones, the Magi. They are following the wild star, the destiny they had never seen before, and they are following it, wherever it goes, to find the King its shining shows them.

The older children now bring forward the three kings as all the people sing verse one of the hymn "We Three Kings."

After the hymn, resume telling the story.

The kings' journey ends in a new kind of king. Their restlessness rests at last. They fall to their knees and give him bright gold, sweet-smelling frankincense and bitter myrrh, brought so far with so much love.

MOVEMENTS

WORDS

So now we all come, following the star, to find God-with-us. We come, as people have come all through the ages, to bring our own gifts to this Child, God's gift to us.

Come forward now. Bring your gifts of stars and of yourselves to place around the manger. Show us the way into the Mystery of Christmas, as we sing, for this night is holy and filled with overflowing silence.

All the children, some accompanied by their parents, now bring forward stars to place in and around the stable as all the people sing verse one of the hymn "Silent Night."

ENRICHMENT LESSON
THE MYSTERY OF CHRISTMAS

LESSON NOTES
FOCUS: THE INCARNATION
- LITURGICAL ACTION
- ENRICHMENT PRESENTATION

THE MATERIAL
- LOCATION: CHRISTMAS SHELVES
- PIECES: PICTURES (MOUNTED ON FOAMCORE OR WOOD) OF THE ANNUNCIATION, VISITATION, NATIVITY, PRESENTATION IN THE TEMPLE, ADORATION OF THE MAGI, MASSACRE OF THE INNOCENTS AND THE FLIGHT INTO EGYPT; LABELS FOR EACH PICTURE, ALSO MOUNTED ON FOAMCORE OR WOOD; ADDITIONAL PIECES OF FOAMCORE OR WOOD ON WHICH YOU HAVE GLUED COPIES OF THE RELATED BIBLICAL TEXTS
- UNDERLAY: WHITE

BACKGROUND

This enrichment lesson can be presented on any Sunday either before or after Christmas, as time allows. The presentation is based on the book *The Glorious Impossible* by Madeleine L'Engle (New York: Simon & Schuster, 1990). Ms. L'Engle provides a poetic commentary on seven classical moments of the infancy narratives of Matthew and Luke. The medieval frescoes of Giotto are used instead of modern, realistic pictures or models to honor the deep mystery of the Incarnation without the loss of its historical fact.

NOTES ON THE MATERIAL

Find the materials for this presentation on the top shelf of the Christmas shelves, placed to the left of the focal shelves. You will find the material to the right of the stand of Advent cards on the top shelf.

This material can be made by the storyteller or other church member. First purchase *two* copies of the book *The Glorious Impossible.* One book will be cut apart to provide pictures. The other book is used as a control and for the children to be able to read Madeliene L'Engle's text to match to the pictures. **Please note:** it is a violation of copyright law to make copies of either the pictures or text from *The Glorious Impossible.* (You can use the remaining portions of the cut-apart book to make additional display materials, if you wish.)

The material is a golden box with a picture of the Madonna and child glued to the lid of the box. (You can find this picture on the endpaper inside the *back* cover of *The Glorious Impossible.*) Glue a picture of Christ the Teacher to the bottom of the box. (You can find this picture on the endpaper inside the *front* cover of *The Glorious Impossible.*) Inside the box you will place plaques made from foamcore or wood. Glue each of these pictures from *The Glorious Impossible* to a separate plaque: the Annunciation, Visitation, Nativity, Adoration of the Magi, Presentation in the Temple, Massacre of the Innocents, and the Flight into Egypt. On the back of each plaque, put dots as a reminder of the correct order in which to show the pictures: one dot for the Annunciation, two dots for the Visitation, and so on, ending with seven dots on the back of the picture of the Flight into Egypt.

On separate but smaller plaques, glue a label that names each picture. On a third set of plaques, glue the related biblical texts.

SPECIAL NOTES

Classroom Management: Finding time for this presentation can be tricky. Some storytellers may prefer to use this during the Advent season. Some use it on the feast of Christ the King, the last Sunday *before* Advent; others use it after Christmas.

As you tell the story, you will hold the picture and turn it so that everyone can see it as you tell about it. It does not usually work to have the children pass the pictures around the circle. Some children will take too long, dominating the circle and your attention, while others will find it hard to wait for each picture. Instead show the pictures yourself, placing the plaques in order in front of you on the underlay as you finish telling about them.

Playing with the Story: This presentation takes advantage of several approaches to learning to speak "Christian." These moves are based on classical Montessori practice and can be used with other lessons as well:

- Nonreaders and those who cannot yet read numbers can try, individually or in groups, to tell the story using the pictures, laying them out on the underlay. When the story is finished, the children then turn over the pictures and count the dots on the back to see if they have the right order. Order in stories is important.

- Both readers and nonreaders can "label" the pictures. This is done by the classical Montessori three-period lesson. First, you read aloud the label, then point to the correct picture and/or place the label beside it. Second, you read aloud or show the label and let the child tell you which picture it refers to. Third, the children name the story and point to the picture and/or place the label.

- More experienced readers can read from *The Glorious Impossible*. After listening to the story as written by L'Engle, the children match that telling of the story to the classical name of the event and to its picture

- Remember that this book has many uses in addition to telling about the Incarnation. It contains the whole story of the Christian People. You can use this approach to create your own lessons.

- This lesson also includes the biblical texts, which are often heard or sung in church around the celebration of the Incarnation. Readers and nonreaders alike can use these. Apply the principles outlined above to set this up.

- Note that in multiple-graded classrooms, nonreaders and readers can work together to enjoy this "inter-play" of word and symbol.

MOVEMENTS

Go to the shelves to get the gold box. Bring it back to the circle and place it in the middle of the circle.

Put the box beside you.

Spread the white underlay. Carefully remove the lid and take out the first picture: the Annunciation.

Place the Annunciation card in front of you to your right, leaving room to eventually lay out all seven pictures in front of you on the white underlay. Then hold out the Visitation card.

Point to the halos around Mary and Elizabeth.

WORDS

Watch carefully where I go, so you always know where to find this lesson.

This is like a parable, but it is bigger than a parable. It is the biggest parable of all, the wonderful impossible. It shows the Incarnation, how God became a baby.

Today I want to show you the whole story. Parts of the Christmas story are not told very often, but they all need to be told, even the sad parts. There are even two births in the whole story! One is the birth of Jesus, and the other is the birth of his cousin, John, the one we know later as John the Baptist.

Look. Do you see what is happening to the mother Mary? This is the Annunciation. The angel Gabriel is announcing to Mary that God has chosen her to be the mother of God.

Do you see Mary? the angel? They have the same colors, but the angel has wings.

Mary was scared, but happy. She was stunned, but blessed.

Mary was a lucky girl, because she had an older friend to talk to. It was Elizabeth. She went to visit her cousin Elizabeth. Elizabeth was much older, maybe even old enough to be Mary's mother. When Mary came close to Elizabeth and greeted her, something wonderful happened.

Elizabeth felt the baby inside her move when he heard Mary's voice. She said something like this, "Blessed are you among women, and blessed is the baby you are going to have. When you spoke, the baby within me jumped. Something wonderful is going to happen with your baby and with mine, too."

When Elizabeth said that, Mary began to sing a song people call "The Magnificat" because it begins, "My soul magnifies the Lord."

Look at the halos. These are the gold circles of light around some of the people. They are the holy ones. The artist used real gold in his paint or beat the gold out very, very thin and pressed it into the paint and plaster to make these gold halos. In this picture, the ones with halos are Mary and Elizabeth.

MOVEMENTS

WORDS

See how Mary is. Look how old Elizabeth looks. The artist wanted us to remember that Elizabeth was too old to have a baby, and was old enough to be a really wise and good friend to Mary.

Place the Visitation card to your left of the Annunciation card and finish telling the story of Elizabeth and Zechariah.

⇒ Wait. Let me finish the story. This is the part of the story that people often leave out, because there is no picture for it. It is about the other baby that was born.

Elizabeth's husband, Zechariah, was a priest. It was his time to work at the Temple, so he went inside to burn the incense and pray.

While Zechariah was at the altar, he glanced over to his right, and there was a bright light. "Don't be afraid," the angel said. Angels are messengers from God, and they are scary. But the angel said, "Don't be afraid. I bring you good news. You and Elizabeth will have a baby."

"But we are too old," Zechariah said, and that was the last thing he said. The angel took away his words. It's not a good idea to argue with an angel. The angel then told Zechariah what the baby's name was supposed to be and disappeared.

Mary stayed three months with Elizabeth and then went home to Nazareth. Elizabeth had her baby. Friends came to help her. When the baby boy was born they all wanted to name him "Zechariah," after his father.

Zechariah shook his head, "No," and then wrote, "The baby's name is John." When they named the baby "John," Zechariah could speak again. It was then that he said his prayer. It is called the "Benedictus" because it is a poem or song of praise that begins: "Blessed be the Lord, the God of Israel." He was so happy!

Pick up the third card: the Nativity. Show it as you talk about it.

⇒ Then Mary's baby was born. That's why this is called "The Nativity," which means "the birth." See how mother Mary is lying down. She is awake and happy, but Joseph is asleep. The baby is wrapped in strips of cloth. These strips are the swaddling cloths or clothes you hear about in the story.

Look at all the angels. They are so happy, they are flying all over and singing the "Gloria in Excelsis." You may have heard this song in church. It sings, "Glory to God in the highest, and on

MOVEMENTS

Place the Nativity card to your left of the first two cards. Take out the fourth card: the Presentation.

Place the Presentation card to your left of the first three cards. Take out the fifth card: the Adoration of the Magi.

WORDS

earth peace, good will among men." When it says "men," it means to all people, boys and girls.

This is another part of the story that is often left out. It is called the Presentation. After a time, Mary and Joseph took their new little baby to the Temple in Jerusalem. It was the custom to present a new baby there to celebrate its name and to dedicate the baby to God.

When Mary and Joseph took the baby into the Temple to be dedicated to God, an old man named Simeon came up and looked at the baby. He took the baby in his arms and said, "Now I can die in peace." What was he talking about?

When Simeon was younger, God told him that he would not die before seeing the Holy One who was coming and would change everything. That day Simeon knew Jesus was the one he had been waiting for.

Then old Anna came up and looked at the baby. She saw that this was the Holy One, too. She gave thanks to God and told everyone in the Temple what had happened.

Simeon is holding the baby. Mary is still holding out her arms. Joseph is bringing two birds to the temple. That was the custom in those days.

Here is old Anna. She loved to be in the temple as much as she could be. I don't know why she doesn't have a halo. Look at her coat. At first, it looks brown and old, but if you look closely, it seems to be all gold.

When old Simeon held the baby, he said a prayer we remember and sometimes sing. It begins, "Lord, now lettest thou thy servant depart in peace."

The three kings, the Magi, the wise men, finally arrived. They were late. Every year, they are late! They are adoring the baby. That means they are just standing there and looking at the baby and enjoying him. They also brought presents.

Look at the star! This is the wild star they have been following.

MOVEMENTS

WORDS

The artist didn't know very much about camels. He knew they had long necks, a hump and long legs, but look at their faces. They look more like donkeys. See their long ears. That doesn't matter. We still know what he was trying to paint.

Place the Adoration of the Magi card to your left of the first four cards. Get out the next card: the Massacre of the Innocents, but don't yet turn it around for the children to see. Because of the terrible events it depicts, this card needs introduction.

This is a part of the story that is often left out, too. It is no wonder people do not tell this part. It is too sad. It is called the Massacre of the Innocents.

The three kings followed the star to the land where Jesus was born. When they came into the land, they went to see the king, King Herod in Jerusalem. When King Herod heard them say they were looking for a baby king, he was very interested. He did not want that baby to grow up. Herod wanted to be the only king in the land.

"Come and tell me when you find this king," he told the Magi. "I want to come and worship him." Herod was not telling the truth. He wanted to kill the new little king.

The three kings, the wise men, did not tell Herod. They went home by another way. They really were wise.

But Herod did not forget. He asked his scholars to look in the scriptures and find where it said the king would be born. They told Herod that the place would be Bethlehem. Herod sent his soldiers there, and they killed every baby boy they could find who was two years old or younger.

Now turn over the picture and hold it out for the children to see.

It was a terrible thing. The mothers and fathers were very sad. You can see that many babies have already been killed. The soldiers took them from their mothers. No one really looks happy in the picture, not even Herod.

Trace the length of the mothers' eyes with your finger.

Look at the mothers' eyes. The artist tried to make them look very, very sad. See how long and narrow they are?

Place the Massacre of the Innocents card down to your left of the first five cards. Take out the seventh card: the Flight into Egypt.

I guess the story is over then, isn't it? No. The baby Jesus did not die in Bethlehem.

An angel came to Joseph in a dream before the soldiers arrived. The angel told Joseph to take his little family to another country. They fled far away to the land of Egypt. Mary and the baby rode on the donkey, and Joseph led the way.

MOVEMENTS

Place the Flight into Egypt card to your left of the first six cards. Sit back and look at the whole series.

Show the children the various ways the pictures, biblical passages and labels can be used. (See Special Notes on p. 57)

When the interplay of labels, Bible passages and pictures is finished, sit back and look at the whole sequence again.

Show the children the picture on the lid of the box, and then the figure inside on the bottom of the box.

Name everything as you put the lesson away in the box. Take your time. When the box is closed, return it to the shelf where you got it. Then help children choose their work.

WORDS

➡ Now let's enjoy the whole story.

➡ Here is the mother Mary. This is God the Father. Joseph was like a father, but the baby was from God.

LESSON 5
EPIPHANY

LESSON NOTES

FOCUS: THE WISE MEN'S GIFTS

- ● LITURGICAL ACTION
- ● CORE PRESENTATION

THE MATERIAL

- ● LOCATION: FOCAL SHELVES AND CHRISTMAS SHELVES
- ● PIECES: ADVENT CARDS ON A RACK OR TRAY; 4 ADVENT CANDLES IN A BOX, MATCHES IN A METAL CONTAINER AND A CANDLE SNUFFER, ALL ON A TRAY; PURPLE OR BLUE CLOTH OR FELT; NATIVITY SET FIGURES OF MARY, JOSEPH, DONKEY, SHEPHERD, SHEEP, WISE MEN, CHRIST CHILD, MANGER; FRANKIN-CENSE, MYRRH, GOLD-COVERED CHOCOLATE COINS; TWEEZERS; MODEL OF BETHLEHEM; OPTIONAL: CANDLE HOLDERS
- ● UNDERLAY: PURPLE AND WHITE

BACKGROUND

Epiphany is a Greek word that means "showing forth." The date of its celebration is January 6th. It was originally concerned with the commemoration of the Baptism of Christ and later became associated with the Magi, an emphasis of the Latin Church of the West. Today it is often thought of as the manifestation of Christ to the Gentiles.

You begin this week's lesson by presenting the four Advent cards and the Christmas card and telling the stories found in Lesson 1 (pp. 27-33), Lesson 2 (pp. 34-39), Lesson 3 (pp. 40-44) and Lesson 4 (pp. 45-51).

NOTES ON THE MATERIAL

You'll find the materials for this presentation on the Christmas shelves and the focal shelves. The model of Bethlehem stands to the far left on the top shelf of the Christmas shelves. In the middle of the top shelf you'll find the tray or rack of Advent cards. The box of candles, container of matches and candle snuffer are on a tray at the left end of the second shelf (below the model of Bethlehem).

A special stand or carrier rack for the Advent cards makes them visible to a child scanning the room. This stand for the cards should also hold the rolled-up underlay. If you do not use this stand, put the rolled-up underlay and cards in a tray. You may want to line the tray with purple or blue cloth or felt.

There are five cards or wooden plaques, representing, in this order:
• the prophets
• the Holy Family
• the shepherds
• the Magi
• the birth of Jesus

These cards or plaques are laid on a strip of cloth divided into five equal sections, one section for each of the four weeks of Advent, plus an additional section for the feast of Christmas. The first four sections of this cloth are purple or blue (for Advent); the fifth and final section is white (for Christmas). This cloth is the Advent underlay; roll up the underlay so that the white segment is hidden inside. (An illustration of the underlay, with all five cards or plaques laid out in order, appears on p. 68.)

Many churches use blue for their Advent color. In this presentation, we refer to the liturgical color purple, but use whatever color your church uses. Instead of referring to the royal color (purple), point out that blue is a good color for getting ready, because it is the color associated with Mary, Jesus' mother. Without the mother Mary, there would be no baby.

You also need a box to hold the four candles used in the lesson. In this presentation, we refer to one rose and three purple candles, but, again, follow the custom of your church. Use candles with wide bases for stability (e.g., votives or pillar candles), or, if you use tapers, also use candle holders. You also need a metal container for matches; look in an import store for beautiful and inexpensive metal containers. Though this container may tarnish quickly, some children may enjoy keeping it polished in the classroom! You will also need a candle snuffer. Keep these items (candles, matches and snuffer) on a tray lined with purple or blue cloth or felt.

You need a model of the city of Bethlehem, similar to that pictured on page 31. It is to be set in the middle of the circle of children to show that we are all on the way to Bethlehem, including the storyteller.

You will need the figures from the Holy Family, which sit in the center of the top shelf of the focal shelves.

Also from the focal shelves, you'll need the Christ Candle, which sits to the left of the Holy Family on the top shelf. This candle will be used in Lesson 6, too, when you tell the story of Baptism.

Finally, you will need to include the gifts of the Magi: lumps of frankincense, lumps of myrrh and gold-covered chocolate coins.

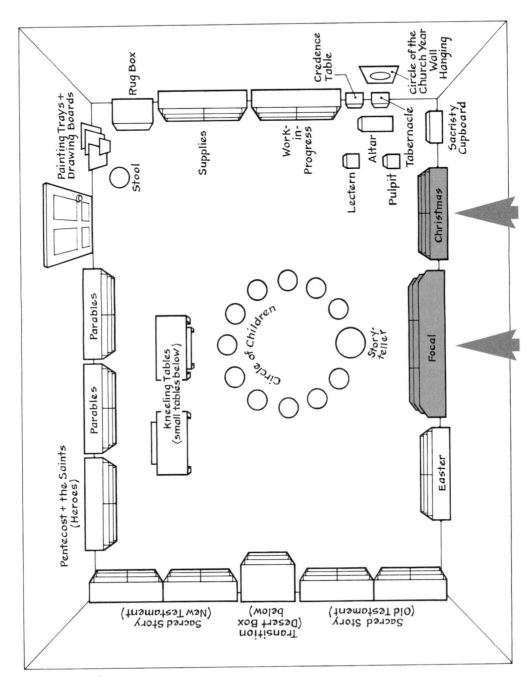

WHERE TO FIND MATERIALS

MOVEMENTS

When the children are ready, go to the Christmas shelves and get the materials you need, as described in Lesson 1, Advent I (p. 30).

Place the first Advent card and tell about the prophets (pp. 30-32). Do not minimize or rush that story. End with the words: "Something incredible is going to happen in Bethlehem."

Place the second Advent card and tell about the Holy Family (pp. 37-38). Do not minimize or rush this story. End with the words: "They must have been the last people coming up the road to Bethlehem that night."

Place the third Advent card and tell about the shepherds (pp. 42-43). Do not minimize or rush this story. End with the words: "Run to Bethlehem to see the child who will change everything."

Place the fourth Advent card and tell about the wise men (pp. 48-49). Do not minimize or rush this story. End with the words: "...because, like us, they too are on the way to Bethlehem."

Place the Christmas card and tell about the birth of Jesus (p. 49). Do not minimize or rush this story. End with the words: "All the old cow could do was look and look at the baby with its big brown eyes."

Place the four Advent candles and the Christ Candle, one by one, between you and the underlay with the five cards on it.

WORDS

Watch carefully where I go so you will always know where to find this lesson.

Here is the candle of the prophets. This is the candle of the Holy Family. Here is the candle of the shepherds. Here is the candle of the wise men. Here is the Christ Candle.

MOVEMENTS

WORDS

Light all five candles in order.

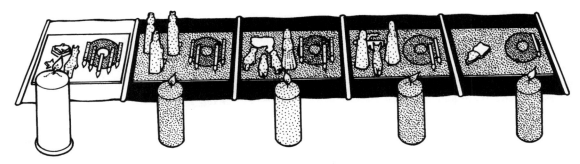

THE ADVENT AND CHRISTMAS CARDS AND CANDLES (STORYTELLER'S PERSPECTIVE)

Return again to the fourth card and candle.

This is the light of the Magi, the kings, the wise men. They brought gifts: frankincense, myrrh and gold.

Show the gold coins.

The gold was for a king, but for a different kind of king, so they also brought frankincense. This is something that was used for worship, then, and it is still used to pray today.

Take out the container of frankincense and open it. Using tweezers, pick up one of the crystals of incense. Place it in the flame of the light of the Magi.

Here is frankincense. Watch. First there is the black smoke, and then when it turns white, the fragrance, the scent, is released. Do you see? Can you begin to smell it?

The incense will bubble and turn black. Keep lighting new pieces if you need to until the children can smell it. This may take some time. Do not let them pass it around, because the tweezers get hot.

When this is completed, you then get out the myrrh and place it in the flame of the king's candle.

This is myrrh. This was not a gift for an ordinary king. This is what is burned at funerals. It is also placed with the dead for their burial. This is for someone whose death is important.

Watch. Do you see the smoke? Can you begin to smell the scent? It is very different from frankincense. Some people like one, and others like the other. They are both important as gifts to show that this king was not to be like other kings. Now let me change the light as we did before.

MOVEMENTS

Take out the candle snuffer from the candle tray.

Snuff out all the candles slowly, starting with the candles of Advent.

Slowly snuff out the Christ Candle.

Enjoy the moment and then begin to put the lesson back. There is no wondering at the end of this lesson.

Replace everything without hurrying. Return to the circle and ask the children what work they would like to get out that day.

WORDS

➠ Now watch. I am going to change the light.

➠ Now I am going to change the light of the Christ Candle. Look. It too is spreading out to fill up the room. As it spreads out, it gets thinner and thinner until you can't see it at all. That doesn't mean that it's gone. It only means that you can't see it. You can still feel Christmas. It is filling up the room with the prophets, the Holy Family, the shepherds and the three kings. Anywhere you go, you can come close to them.

➠ Now watch carefully where I go with this material, so you will always know where to get it when you want to work with it.

LESSON 6
HOLY BAPTISM

LESSON NOTES
FOCUS: INITIATION BY WATER AND THE HOLY SPIRIT

- LITURGICAL ACTION
- CORE PRESENTATION

THE MATERIAL

- LOCATION: FOCAL SHELVES
- PIECES: LARGE TRAY HOLDING A BOWL (FOR THE BAPTISMAL FONT), PITCHER OF WATER, DOVE, CONTAINER OF FRAGRANT OIL, METAL BOX OF MATCHES, CANDLE SNUFFER AND WHITE UNDERLAYS; BASKET HOLDING A BABY DOLL, WRAPPED IN WHITE BLANKET OR GOWN; BRASS BOWL OF SAND; BASKET OF CANDLES, WITH DRIP GUARDS (OR CANDLES WITH HOLDERS); CHRIST CANDLE
- UNDERLAY: 3 WHITE FELT CIRCLES

BACKGROUND

You can present this lesson at any time during the Church year, but it is especially appropriate on the First Sunday after Epiphany (January 6), a Sunday known as the Baptism of Our Lord, or on any Sunday when a baptism is celebrated.

Holy Baptism is full initiation by water and the Holy Spirit into the Church. The rite draws both the past and future into the present, so there is no need to be baptized more than once. For Christians, this rite is the gateway into the family of families we call the Church. It remains the primary moment in the life of a Christian person to be remembered and looked forward to.

We baptize people in the traditional name of the Holy Trinity—Father, Son and Holy Spirit—so the primary material used in this lesson is three overlapping white circles, a well-known symbol of the Trinity. The names of Creator, Redeemer and Sustainer are juxtaposed to the classical language to show that the Trinity is about much more than gender.

We place images of action on each of the white circles: the pouring of water for the Creator, the lighting of the Christ Candle for the Redeemer, and the images of dove and the invisible scent of oil for the Sustainer. We ask children to remember or look forward to the day of their baptism by lighting candles from the light of the Christ Candle, since this is also the day they receive their "light."

NOTES ON THE MATERIAL

On a large tray place three rolled-up, white felt circles (each about 18" in diameter), a glass bowl (for the font, about 8" in diameter), a pitcher of water, a three-dimensional figure of a dove (about 5" in length), a small bottle or vial of fragrant oil, a metal box of matches and a candle snuffer. In a basket you need to have a baby doll, wrapped in a white blanket or dressed in a white gown. You also need a brass bowl (about 8" in diameter) half filled with sand and a second basket holding small candles (about ½" in diameter and 4" tall) fitted with drip guards, to protect the children's hands from hot wax. For children too small to handle candles, provide candles (tapers or votives) in holders, one to place in front of each child. You will also need the Christ Candle.

Find the materials for this presentation on the focal shelves. The Christ Candle sits on the top focal shelf, to the left. The tray of materials and basket with the doll are on the middle focal shelf, directly underneath the Christ Candle (to the left). The basket of small candles and bowl of sand are on the bottom focal shelf, underneath the other baptism materials (to the left).

Adapt the materials according to the usage of your church. For example, if your church uses a shell for baptism, you can place one on the tray with the other materials. If your tradition baptizes by total immersion, you will need to work out a way to show that, perhaps using a larger bowl or basin as the font instead of the bowl described above.

SPECIAL NOTES

Classroom Management: When the lesson about Holy Baptism is presented to the children, it is not a baptism, nor is it playing at baptism. Instead, the lesson invites children to "remember the day of their baptism or look forward to the day of their baptism." Thus we use a doll rather than a real person.

Cleaning supplies for the children to use should include polishing materials. Children will enjoy polishing the metal parts of the materials used in today's presentation. Some children will want to choose polishing for their individual work.

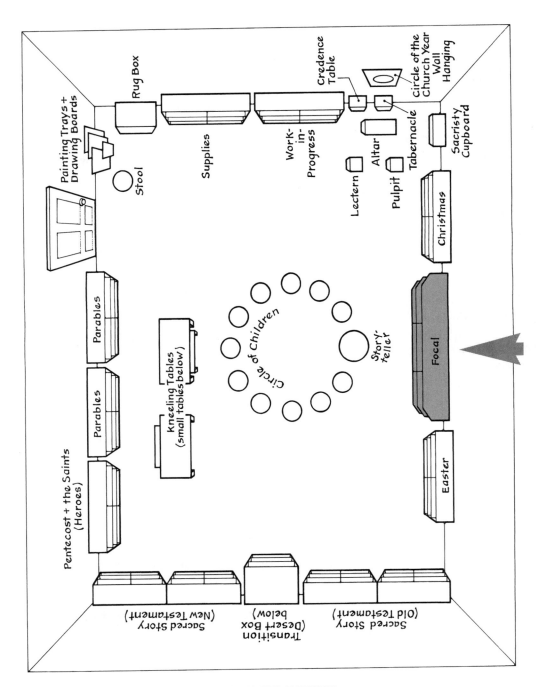

WHERE TO FIND MATERIALS

MOVEMENTS

Before the lesson, fill the pitcher with water and check the matches. Will they strike?

When the children are settled, get up and walk around the room. Then come back to where you were seated, in front of the focal shelves.

The Baptism materials are on the lower focal shelves, beneath the Christ Candle, which is on the left of the top focal shelf.

Bring to the circle the large tray, the two baskets and the bowl with sand in it. Place these on either side of where you will be sitting.

Get the Christ Candle. When you are settled and when the children are ready, begin.

Unroll the first white circle. Smooth it out. Unroll the second circle and place it so that it smoothly overlaps the first. Unroll the third one and place it so that it smoothly overlaps the first two circles.

Sit back and appreciate this symbol of the Trinity. Then point to each circle and name them again.

Place the pitcher and the glass bowl on the Father circle, the Christ Candle on the Son circle, and the dove and oil on the Holy Spirit circle. Do this slowly and with deliberation.

WORDS

⟩ Watch. Watch where I go to get this lesson. Here are the Sacred Stories. Here are the parables. Here are liturgical action lessons.

⟩ Oh. This is the lesson about Baptism.

⟩ We need something else.

⟩ We baptize people in the name of the Father...the Son...and the Holy Spirit.

⟩ The Creator, the Redeemer, the Sustainer.

MOVEMENTS	WORDS

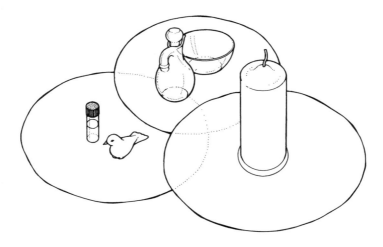

THE THREE CIRCLES OF THE TRINITY (STORYTELLER'S PERSPECTIVE)

Pour the water into the glass bowl, listening to the sound of the water. Then put your hand in the water and move it as you begin to name it. Then cup your hand to draw out some water and pour it back as you continue.

This is the water of creation, the dangerous water of the flood, the water the people went through into freedom, the water Jesus was baptized in, the water you were—or will be—baptized in, and so much more.

When you have contemplated this for a moment, take a match from its container and point to the Christ Candle.

There was once someone who said such wonderful things and did such amazing things that people just had to ask him who he was. One time when they asked him who he was, he said...

Strike the match and light the Christ Candle.

"...I am the Light."

Take the stopper from the container of oil. Move the container slowly around the circle so children can catch its fragrance.

The Holy Spirit goes where it will. It rides the invisible wind like a dove and comes to us when we need its comfort and power. It is invisible, like the scent of this oil. It is invisible but still there.

People are baptized when they are babies, or children, or teenagers, or grownups, or when they are very old. We will use a baby doll to see how this is done.

Pick up the doll and hold it in your arms.

We ask the person about to be baptized questions, or if it's a baby too little to answer, we ask the parents or godparents. We say prayers for them. Then we are ready.

MOVEMENTS	WORDS
	But wait. What is the name of this child? Names are very important in baptism.
Take the first name you get and quickly move on.	"Bobby." That's a good name.
Stir the water and put it on the doll's head, or pour some on, or immerse the doll.	Bobby, I baptize you in the name of the Father...and of the Son...and of the Holy Spirit. Amen.
Put some of the oil on your fingers or thumb and make the sign of the cross on the doll's forehead, if that is your church's custom.	Bobby, you are sealed by the Holy Spirit in baptism and marked as Christ's own forever. Amen.
Carefully place the doll back in its basket. Then, pick up a candle from the candle basket.	This is the day when Bobby receives her light. We light it from the Christ Candle.

Name this child. |
When you or the children respond, "Bobby," continue.	Bobby, remember the day of your baptism.
Light Bobby's candle and place it in the bowl of sand. Pick up another candle from the candle basket to use for yourself.	Name this child. *(Say your own name.)* Remember the day of your baptism.
Place your candle in the bowl of sand. Pass the basket of candles so each child can have one. Repeat the naming and candle-lighting ritual for each child. The children can hold the lit candles, or, if they are not ready for this responsibility, can place them in the bowl of sand.	
As the candles are being lit, call the children's attention to the expanding circle of light.	Look. The light is growing bigger and bigger. Look here. The light that all the light is coming from is not growing smaller. I wonder how so much light can come from one light?

See. Look at all this light. |

MOVEMENTS

Pick up the candle snuffer.

Slowly place the candle snuffer over the flame. Hold it down until the flame is out. Raise the candle snuffer slowly and allow the smoke to rise and expand into the room.

The children take turns changing their light. Then pass the candle basket again so the children can place the extinguished candles in it. Finally, change the light of the Christ Candle.

Some children may not want to change their lights. They can leave them lit by placing them in the sand of the bowl (if they have not already done so). During the session, the candles will melt down and form a single candle with several wicks still flickering with light.

You can omit the wondering after this lesson. The lesson itself holds enormous wonder, and it is somewhat long. Put everything carefully back on the tray and in the baskets. Return the materials to the appropriate shelves. Carry the bowl of sand to the top shelf beside the Christ Candle if there are candles still burning in it. Otherwise, you can replace it on the lowest shelf.

Often there will be no time for a work period after this lesson, so you may proceed directly to the feast.

WORDS

Now let me show you something. Let's change the light. No. I did not say we were going to put it out or extinguish it. Watch. I will show you with mine first.

Do you see how all the light is right here in the flame? It is easy to see then. Now watch. It changes.

See? The light is still spreading out. It is filling up the room. Just because you can't see it anymore doesn't mean that it is gone. Anywhere you go in the room today, there it will be. Our room will be full of invisible light. Your light. The light you received on the day of your Baptism or the light you will receive.

If you don't want to change your light, you may come forward very carefully and put your candle in the sand.

PARABLE OF THE GOOD SHEPHERD

LESSON NOTES

FOCUS: THE SHEPHERD AND HIS SHEEP (MATTHEW 18:12–14; LUKE 15:1–7)

- PARABLE
- CORE PRESENTATION

THE MATERIAL

- LOCATION: PARABLE SHELVES
- PIECES: PARABLE BOX WITH GREEN DOT, 12 BROWN FELT STRIPS, 3 BLACK FELT SHAPES, 1 BLUE FELT SHAPE, 5 SHEEP, 1 GOOD SHEPHERD, 1 ORDINARY SHEPHERD, 1 WOLF
- UNDERLAY: GREEN

BACKGROUND

The primary sheep and shepherd parable of Jesus, recognized as authentic by many scholars, is the shepherd who searches for the one sheep that is lost and leaves the ninety-nine to do so. In this presentation, the gate is left open as the shepherd searches for the sheep, but you will also find that many of life's conflicts find meaning and resolution in the themes from Psalm 23 and John 10, also present in the lesson.

The term *parable* can have a wide meaning. This lesson is more of an identity statement of Jesus than a parable. It is especially connected to and an introduction for the later lessons on the "I am" statements in John's gospel.

NOTES ON THE MATERIAL

Find the material in a gold parable box with a green dot, located on the top shelf of one of the parable shelves. Inside the box is a green underlay with roughly rounded corners and an irregular, approximately square outline. Twelve brown felt strips (about 1" x 10") form the sheepfold. Three irregular black shapes made of felt give the rough appearance of a mouth and two eyes when put together to form the dangerous place. A blue piece of felt provides the water. There are five sheep of different shades of gray and brown, a Good Shepherd, an ordinary shepherd and a wolf.

SPECIAL NOTES

Classroom Management: The parable, as presented here, has served children well since about 1974. Much of its testing came from working with sick children in the hospitals of the Texas Medical Center in Houston from about 1974–1984. It has continued to comfort, challenge and give voice to existential issues. When the child is ready to discuss the open gate, this parable provides the occasion to do so.

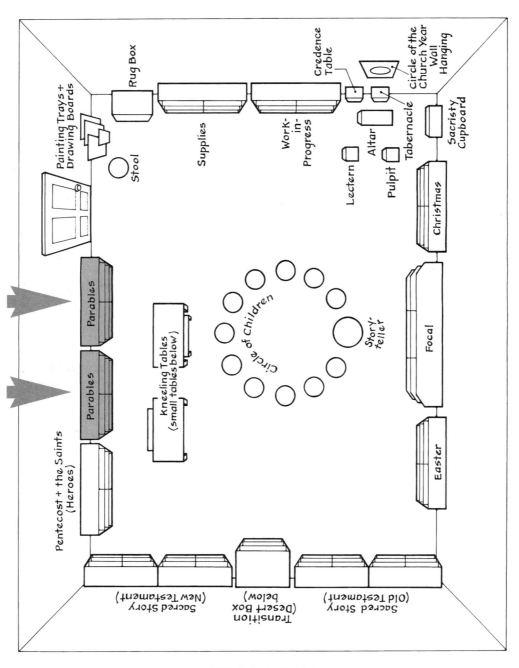

WHERE TO FIND MATERIALS

MOVEMENTS

Go to the parable shelves and bring the gold box to the circle. As you pick up the box, point to the green dot on it. This hint of the underlay's color is the only outside indication of what parable is inside. This prevents giving one parable value over another one by color, size or shape. The children can approach the parables as equals and find the one that is right for them.

Place the box in the middle of the circle.

When you mention the box being closed, knock on the top of the box like a door. When you are talking about the parable being a present, you hold the box out toward the children like you were giving it to them. You might also mention that the parable is old and the box even looks old. You don't need to do all of these opening comments every time.

Sit back. Reflect on the need to be ready to open a parable and to keep from breaking it. When you and the children are ready, you begin.

Carefully move the box back to your side. Remove the lid and leave it tipped up against the box on the circle side. This helps keep the children from being distracted by what is inside.

As you take things out of the box, wonder with the children about what each thing might be. You are inviting the children to help you build the metaphor of the parable, helping create a common ownership in what is to come.

WORDS

Watch carefully where I go so you will always know where to find this lesson.

Look! It is the color gold. Something inside must be precious like gold. Perhaps there is a parable inside. Parables are even more valuable than gold, so maybe there is one inside.

The box is also closed. There is a lid. Maybe there is a parable inside. Sometimes, even if we are ready, we can't enter a parable. Parables are like that. Sometimes they stay closed.

The box looks like a present. Parables were given to you long ago as presents. Even if you don't know what a parable is, the parable is already yours. You don't have to take them, or buy them, or get them in any way. They already belong to you.

You need to be ready to find out if there is a parable inside. It is easy to break parables. What is hard to do is go inside.

I have an idea. Let's look inside and see what's there!

MOVEMENTS

Take out the green underlay. First leave it crumpled. Then smooth it out in the middle of the circle of children.

The idea is to invite many serious and sometimes funny—but not disruptive—responses. This supports ownership in the imagined parable, but it also frustrates the idea that children already know what it is. Some will have already seen this parable many times.

Look up at the imaginary tree.

Turn it over. Smooth it out again. You might do this more than once.

Take from the box the piece of blue felt and place it to your far left on the green underlay. Smooth it out.

Bend over and look into the "window" or "mirror."

Next, take from the box the three pieces of black felt. Hold each piece in the palms of your hands and show them to the children before placing each one on your far right on the part of the underlay nearest the children. The longer strip is placed opposite the two smaller ones, so the sheep can pass between the long one on one side and the two smaller ones on the other side.

WORDS

I wonder what this could really be? It is certainly green. Green. There is nothing here but green.

I wonder if this could be one of those things that frogs sit on in a pond? *(Children will fill in the name if they know it.)*

I wonder if this could be the top of a tree?

I wonder if this could be a leaf from a giant tree? It would have to be really tall.

Yes, it is a piece of cloth, but I wonder what is on the other side?

See, there is always the other side.

I wonder what this could really be?

I wonder if this could be a place to look through to the other side?

I wonder if it is one of those things you look into and see your own face.

Look, there is no light in there at all. I wonder what they could really be? I wonder if they are so deep that the light cannot get there? It's like holding a shadow in your hand.

MOVEMENTS	WORDS
	Sometimes people who sit over there think they see a face. Oh, there is no light in the eyes. There is no light in the smile.
When the wondering about the black pieces of felt is about to conclude, take out a single brown strip and lay it close to you along your bottom right of the underlay. You can walk your fingers along it to suggest a path. Try to stretch it like a rubber band.	I wonder what this could be? A path? A flat log? A stick? No, it is not a rubber band.
The second strip is placed parallel to the first one, but further from you on the overlay.	Here's another one. Maybe the path is in between.
The third piece is placed to the left to connect the first two parallel pieces. It could suggest goal posts for football.	Here's another one. Look. Football? The goal posts? I wonder if it is a bridge between the two paths?
When the figure is closed it looks like a square, but it also could look like a diamond for playing baseball.	Here's another one. Baseball? Now there is an inside and an outside.
Move one of the four strips to suggest the movement of a gate, then lay it flat again to make the square or diamond.	Let's make a gate, so if there is someone inside he or she can go outside. Or someone outside can go inside.
Lay the other strips on top of the strips already laid down, so that you build up the shape you have made to a depth of three strips each.	There are more. It is getting stronger. I wonder what this could really be? Yes, it could be a house, a kind of flat house, but everything's flat in the parable. It could be a place for animals or people. I wonder who lives there?
Take a single sheep out of the box and place it in the sheepfold. Take out the remaining four sheep, one by one. When you are wondering how many there really are, take one away, then another, until there is only one. As you begin to wonder if there are more, you place the sheep back into the sheepfold until all five are back.	Oh, it's a place for sheep. I wonder how many sheep there really are. This many? This many? This many? This many? Maybe only this many? Or maybe there are this many and more.

MOVEMENTS   **WORDS**

THE SHEEP IN THE SHEEPFOLD (STORYTELLER'S PERSPECTIVE)

You are now ready to begin the parable. The building of the metaphor is completed. Sit back and reflect for a moment. Then begin with added focus.

There was once someone who said such amazing things and did such wonderful things that people followed him. They couldn't help it. They wanted to know who he was, so they just had to ask him.

When you say, "I am the Good Shepherd," take the Good Shepherd from the gold box and hold it in the palms of your hands. Show it to the children by moving your hands from one side to the other. Then place the Good Shepherd to your right of the sheepfold between the sheepfold and the edge of the green underlay.

Once when they asked him who he was, he said, "I am the Good Shepherd."

As you begin to speak, lay back part of the sheepfold (to open the gate). Move the Good Shepherd to your left on the underlay. Then move the sheep, one by one, slowly out of the sheepfold into the grass. They move

"I know each one of the sheep by name. When I take them from the sheepfold they follow me. I walk in front of the sheep to show them the way."

MOVEMENTS

WORDS

in single file. Move the first one, then the others so they catch up one by one.

Move your hand over the grass to the left of the sheepfold.

➤ "I show them the way to the good grass..."

Moving the sheep needs to be a slow, fluid movement. Focus on each one as you move them to the piece of blue felt.

➤ "...and I show them the way to the cool, still, fresh water."

Move the Good Shepherd between the black pieces of felt and then begin to move the sheep through. Remember the times you have had to go through danger and let those feelings come into your awareness.

➤ "When there are places of danger..."

Move the sheep through one at a time. Move them slowly. They do not want to go. They turn this way and that. Finally, each one is through but one. Place that last and lost sheep under one of the pieces of black felt with only the head showing.

➤ "...I show them how to go through."

There is silence while the sheep go through. Be comfortable with it.

Bring the four sheep just to the door of the sheepfold. The Good Shepherd is back in the position he started from.

Move each sheep into the sheepfold. You nod your head and silently count each one. The children may join you.

➤ "I count each one as the sheep goes inside."

You then move your hand as if the lost sheep is going in. Clearly that sheep is not there. You look under and above your hand. Where could it be?

➤ "If one of the sheep is missing I would go anywhere to look for the lost sheep..."

MOVEMENTS	WORDS
Move the Good Shepherd in front of the sheepfold and then slowly to the grass, to the water, and through the dangerous place. The gate to the sheepfold is left open.	"...in the grass, by the water, even in places of danger."
Take the sheep from behind the felt piece and tuck it in behind the shoulders of the Good Shepherd. If your Good Shepherd already has a sheep on his back, don't worry. That seldom bothers the children. They will speak up if it does, and you can say, "There's really only one."	"And when the lost sheep is found I would put it on my back, even if it is heavy, and carry it back safely to the sheepfold."
Move the Good Shepherd and the lost sheep through the dangerous place toward the sheepfold. Remove the lost sheep and leave it in front of the sheepfold. Place the Good Shepherd back in his original position. Move the lost sheep into the sheepfold and close the gate.	"When all the sheep are safe inside, I am so happy that I can't be happy just by myself, so I invite all of my friends and we have a great feast."
Sit back and pause. Older children sometimes say, "Sure, and they ate the sheep!" Take that very seriously. Take your time. "You know, the sheep die every time, but the feast is about finding."	
Put the Good Shepherd in the box and take out the ordinary shepherd. Hold this figure in the palm of your hand. Show it to the children and then place the figure on the underlay midway between the water, the dangerous place and the sheepfold.	This is the ordinary shepherd. When the ordinary shepherd takes the sheep from the sheepfold, he does not always show the way.
Move the sheep slowly out of the sheepfold so that one goes to the right, one to the left, one to the far right, one to the far left, and the fifth one goes past the ordinary shepherd toward the far edge of the underlay.	The sheep wander.

MOVEMENTS	WORDS
Take the wolf from the box and show it to the children, as you have the other figures. Place it by the dangerous place facing toward the sheep.	When the wolf comes, the ordinary shepherd runs away...
Move the ordinary shepherd off the underlay to your near left and place him in the box.	
Take the Good Shepherd from the box and place it between the wolf and the sheep. Put it down firmly and leave your hand on it for a moment to establish the strength of this move.	...but the Good Shepherd stays between the wolf and the sheep and would even give his life for the sheep...
Turn each sheep slowly around so each one faces the sheepfold.	...so they can come back safely to the sheepfold.
You then move each one slowly back inside and close the gate.	
Place the Good Shepherd back in his starting place beside the sheepfold. Put the wolf back in the box.	
Sit back and reflect for a moment on the whole parable. You are preparing to lead the wondering, so you need to be in a wondering frame of mind first.	Now, I wonder if these sheep have names?
Point to the sheepfold.	I wonder if the sheep are happy inside this place? I wonder where this place could really be? I wonder if you have ever come close to such a place?
Move your hand over the good grass to your near left.	I wonder if you have ever found the good grass? I wonder if you have ever had the cool, clear, fresh water touch you? I wonder if you ever had to go through a place of danger? I wonder how you got through?

MOVEMENTS

WORDS

I wonder if you have ever been lost?

I wonder if you have ever been found?

I wonder if the Good Shepherd has ever called your name?

As the wondering begins to slow down, you need to be alert, because you want to end the wondering with some energy still in it.

I wonder where this whole place could really be?

When the wondering is over you then begin to place each one of the objects back into the parable box with great care. Do not hurry. You do not know what feelings these pieces of the parable have been invested with. Name the pieces as they are returned to the box.

Here is the Good Shepherd.
Look. The sheep.
The water.
The dangerous place.
The sheepfold.
The grass.

When all is put away you then return the parable box to its place on the parable shelves and begin to help the children decide what work they are going to get out.

Now, I wonder what work you would like to get out today?

LESSON 8
PARABLE OF THE GOOD SAMARITAN

LESSON NOTES

FOCUS: THE SAMARITAN AND THE WOUNDED TRAVELER (LUKE 10:30-35)

● PARABLE

● CORE PRESENTATION

THE MATERIAL

● LOCATION: PARABLE SHELVES

● PIECES: PARABLE BOX WITH DARK BROWN DOT, LIGHT BROWN FELT ROAD, 2 BLACK FELT PIECES, 2 CITY SHAPES, 6 PEOPLE (1 INJURED PERSON, 2 THIEVES, 1 PRIEST, 1 LEVITE, 1 SAMARITAN), 1 "COVERING PIECE" (A PICTURE OF THE SAMARITAN HELPING AN INJURED PERSON)

● UNDERLAY: BROWN BURLAP

BACKGROUND

This parable is found only in Luke 10:30–35. The lawyer's question about the greatest commandment which frames the parable also appears in Mark (12:28–34) and in Matthew (22:34–40), but without the Samaritan.

NOTES ON THE MATERIAL

Find the material in a gold parable box with a dark brown dot, located on the top shelf of one of the parable shelves. Inside the box is a brown underlay, rough and irregularly shaped. There is a lighter brown strip for the road and two black pieces of felt, one for each side of the road. At each end of the road is an abstract city. The outline of Jerusalem has the temple in its appropriate place.

The figures you will use include the person who was injured, the two thieves, the priest, the Levite and the Samaritan. One additional item is called the "covering piece"; it is a picture showing the Samaritan with his donkey as the Samaritan puts a coat on the injured person. This piece is large enough to cover the two figures used on the road. You will place the covering piece over the Samaritan and the injured person, then move the Samaritan and the hurt person together with this covering piece toward Jericho.

SPECIAL NOTES

Classroom Management: The violent events of this parable can sometimes disturb children. Di Pagels, an experienced Godly Play storyteller, recalls a time when one boy turned to another and pushed him hard, saying, "That's what *I'd* do." Instead of focusing on the child's disruption, Di paused in her storytelling, raised her eyes to all the children and said, "I wonder how it felt for that man to be hurt by the robbers." She gave the boy and the entire group an opportunity to enter with more empathy into the feelings of the wounded, and the disruption passed.

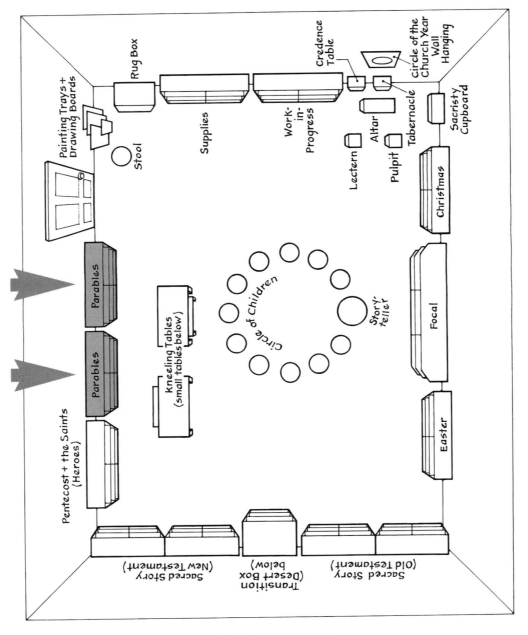

WHERE TO FIND MATERIALS

MOVEMENTS

Go to the parable shelves and pick up the gold parable box. Point to the dark brown circle on the box, which signifies that this is the parable of the Good Samaritan.

Bring the box to the circle and place it in the middle of the circle. Sit back, and begin when you and the children are ready.

Knock on the top of the box as if the top were a door.

Sit back again. Continuing reflecting on what might be in the box.

Move the box to your side and take the lid off. Lean the lid on the side of the box toward the circle so the children cannot see into the box. This increases the mystery and decreases the distraction of what is about to come out of the box for most of those in the circle. You may need to ask the child sitting next to the box if it will bother him or her to have it there. They sometimes begin to announce what is coming, which breaks everyone's concentration.

WORDS

Watch carefully where I go so you will always know where to find this lesson.

You need to be very careful when you come close to a parable. You need to be ready. You can break a parable if you aren't ready.

Look. The box is the color gold. Perhaps there is something valuable like gold inside. There could be a parable inside. They are very valuable. They are worth even more than gold.

The box also has a lid on it. Sometimes it is as if parables have doors that are shut. You can't go inside the parable even if you are ready. I don't know why. It just happens, so don't be discouraged. Keep coming back again and again. One day the parable will open up for you.

The box looks like a present. You know, there may be a parable inside, because you were given parables as a present, even before you were born. Even if you don't know what a parable is, it is still yours.

It looks old. Parables are also old. They are older than you, and they are older than me. They are even older than your grandmother or grandfather. They are almost two thousand years old.

I wonder if there really is a parable inside? I have an idea. Let's look and see.

Hmmm. I wonder what this could be?

MOVEMENTS

Remove the brown underlay. Drop it in a crumpled shape in the middle of the circle and look at it for a moment. Then, begin to smooth it out.

Wait for the children to begin to wonder. If they do not begin, you might suggest a few things like a giant cookie or a piece of wood to get them started. See if you can leave dirt or the desert for them to propose. If there is silence, let there be silent for awhile. It is important for the children to know that silence is important and no cause for anxiety.

Wait a moment and then turn to the box and bring out the "road." Lay the road from one corner to the other, starting at your near left.

The children may see the new piece as a road or a river. It might be a fence you have to jump over. (Move your fingers along and jump them over it.) There are many things it might be. Invite the children to help you build the metaphor of the parable so it will be the common property of all.

Place Jerusalem and then Jericho at opposite ends of the road. Make sure Jerusalem is at the end nearest you.

Take the two black pieces of felt from the box one at a time. Put one on one side of the road and the other on the other side of the road at the midpoint of the road.

WORDS

I wonder what this could really be? There is so much brown. There is no green at all. Look, there is no blue. There is nothing but brown, and the brown is scratchy.

It is hard to know what this could really be if there is only brown. Let's see if there is anything else in the box that can help us.

Now, I wonder what this could be? What could it really be? Yes. It could be a crack. Perhaps the whole thing is going to break into two pieces?

Let's see if there is anything else to help us. Oh, look. It is a road. It is going from this place to this place. But there is more. Look at this.

I wonder what these could be? There is no light in them at all. They are like shadows. Let's see what else there is to help us make the parable.

MOVEMENTS   ## WORDS

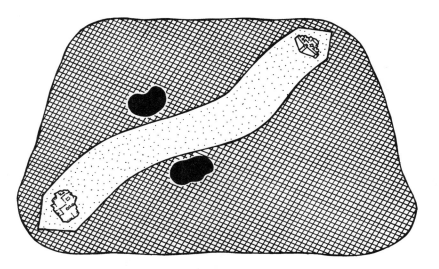

JERUSALEM AND JERICHO (STORYTELLER'S PERSPECTIVE)

Take out the two thieves and put one behind each of the black felt pieces by the road. Sit back and prepare. When you and the children are ready, you begin.

There was once someone who did such amazing things and said such wonderful things that people followed him. As they followed him they heard him speaking of many things. Sometimes people asked him questions.

One day a person asked him what the most important thing in life is. The person he asked said, "You already know."

"That is true. I do. It is to love God and to love people just like they are your neighbors." The person paused a while and thought. He then asked another question, "But who is my neighbor?"

The person he asked then told this parable.

Take the person out of the box who is making the journey and place him at the Jerusalem end of the road by you. Begin to move him slowly along the road, toward the children, as you speak.

There was once someone who went from Jerusalem down to Jericho. As he went along his way he was attacked by robbers. They hurt him, took everything that he had, and left him by the side of the road half dead.

MOVEMENTS

Take the robbers out from behind the "rocks" and placed them in an "X" over the traveler. Then move the robbers off the underlay, back to the box or to your side. When you say "half dead" you turn over the traveler. He is at the side of the road by one of the "rocks."

Move the priest from Jerusalem slowly down the middle of the road. Don't hurry.

When the priest comes to the injured traveler, move the priest slowly to the other side of the road and past the traveler. When the priest is past, move him back into the middle of the road and on to Jericho. Move the priest off the underlay.

Move the Levite slowly down the road. When he comes to the injured traveler, move the Levite to the other side of the road and past the traveler. When the Levite has passed the traveler, move him back into the middle of the road and off the underlay.

Move the Samaritan slowly down the road until he comes to the injured traveler.

Move the Samaritan to the traveler.

WORDS

There was also a great priest of the temple who went on the road from Jerusalem down to Jericho. As he went along his way he came to the place where the person was who had been hurt, had everything taken from him, and had been left by the side of the road half dead.

When the priest came to him, the priest went to the other side and went along his way.

There was also someone else who worked at the temple who went from Jerusalem down to Jericho. He was one of the people who helped the priests. He took care of the temple and helped with the music. He was called a Levite.

When the Levite came to the place where the person was who had been hurt, had everything taken from him, and had been left by the side of the road half dead, he went to the other side, and he went along his way.

There also was a person who went on the road who did not live in Jerusalem. He was visiting from a country called Samaria. The people in Samaria did not like the people in Jerusalem, and the people in Jerusalem did not like the people from Samaria.

When the stranger came to where the person was who had been hurt, had everything taken from him, and had been left by the side of the road half dead, the stranger went to him.

MOVEMENTS

Then reach into the box and take out the "covering piece" that shows the Samaritan putting a coat on the injured traveler. Put the card over the figures of the Samaritan and the traveler.

WORDS

The stranger put medicine on the places where the person was hurt. He gave him his coat to put on. He then put him on his donkey and took him to a place to spend the night.

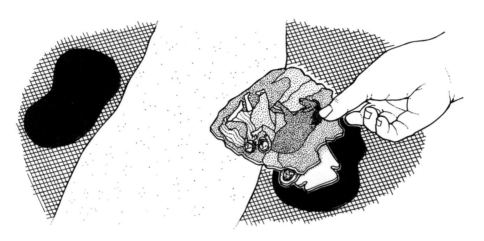

PLACING THE "COVERING PIECE" (STORYTELLER'S PERSPECTIVE)

Move the stranger and the traveler with the card over them along the road almost all the way to Jericho.

The stranger even stayed with him all the night, and in the morning he gave the innkeeper enough money for him to stay there until he was well.

Sit back and ponder the whole parable. While you are doing this, line up the figures to your left on the underlay closest to you. Put the traveler farther away from you and the other figures, but also on the underlay. You are going to place different figures beside the traveler and ask who is the neighbor.

Now I wonder, who is the neighbor to the person who was hurt, had everything taken from him, and was left by the side of the road half dead?

Place the priest beside the traveler. Ask the first question. Wait. Repeat for the Levite and the thieves. Finally place the Samaritan. The children may disagree, but usually there is no question about who the neighbor is. You then go on.

I wonder if it could be this one? This one? Could it be this one? I wonder if it could be this one?

MOVEMENTS

Move the traveler to join the other figures at your near left. Put one of the robbers in the place where the traveler was. Move the priest up beside the robber. Try the Levite. Some may have already asked you to try the other robber. The Samaritan needs to be tried. The one that may create the most discussion is the traveler.

Move the priest down to the comparison position. Some will think the Levite has to be his neighbor since he works for him. Much discussion will follow.

Try different combinations of the figures, always asking:

When you have tried all of the combinations of the figures, turn to this final bit of wondering. All of the figures are still laid out on the underlay.

When the wondering about the change of men to women begins to subside, wonder about children. The children need to know that going to get help is also helping.

Pick up each figure, one at a time, and carefully place them back in the box. Put the road and the dark pieces in the box, then fold up the underlay and place it in the box, too.

Walk slowly to the parable shelves and return the parable box to its proper place. Help the children decide what work they will get out during the response time.

WORDS

I wonder who is the neighbor to this one? Ahh. That's not easy, is it? Could it be this one? How about this one? This one?

Who is the neighbor to this one?

Who is the neighbor to this one?

Now I wonder what would happen if the people in the parable were women and not men?

I wonder what would happen if the person finding the injured traveler were a child?

Here is the traveler.
The Samaritan.
The priest.
The Levite.
The two thieves.
The rocks.
The city and the inn.
The road.

Now watch carefully where I go, so you will always know where to get this parable.

PARABLE OF THE GREAT PEARL

LESSON NOTES

FOCUS: THE MERCHANT AND THE GREAT PEARL (MATTHEW 13:45)

- PARABLE
- CORE PRESENTATION

THE MATERIAL

- LOCATION: PARABLE SHELVES
- PIECES: PARABLE BOX WITH WHITE DOT, 5 BROWN RECTANGULAR PLACES, 2 FIGURES (MERCHANT AND SELLER), MERCHANT'S POSSESSIONS (MONEY, CHEST, BED, CANDLE, VASE, CHAIR, FOOTSTOOL)
- UNDERLAY: WHITE

BACKGROUND

In the canonical gospels, this parable is found only in Matthew 13:45. Another version of the parable can be found in the Gospel of Thomas (Gospel of Thomas, 76).

NOTES ON THE MATERIAL

Find the material in a gold parable box with a white dot, located on the top shelf of one of the parable shelves. Inside the box is a white underlay in the shape of a circle. There are two figures, the seller, shown sitting at a table, and the merchant.

Five brown, felt rectangular "outline" shapes of various sizes represent houses, villages, countries, worlds—living places or other realities. These shapes are empty, with an opening in each one. Inside one shape, place the seller at a table.

Inside another outline shape, place an assortment of goods: a bed, a chest, bags of gold, chair, footstool, a candle, a vase and other things. These are the possessions which the merchant will exchange for the great pearl.

A little gold box contains three pearls, each one a different size. (Placing cotton in the box helps show that the pearls are important.) As you lay out the story, you will place one pearl on the table in the seller's place and two other pearls in two of the remaining empty shapes. One outline shape remains entirely empty.

SPECIAL NOTES

Storytelling Tip: When you tell the story, you may be tempted to use the largest pearl for the great pearl. Choose a different pearl instead, because greatness has to do with more than size. Be prepared for the children's wondering to touch upon this issue. Children often regard big things as more important than small; for example, they might feel that adults are more important than children. Furthermore, our culture holds up big things for us to admire, too, from big houses to big cars and big bank accounts.

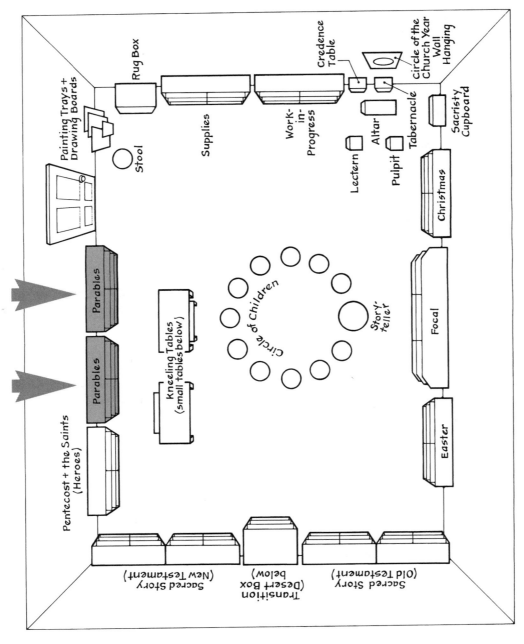

WHERE TO FIND MATERIALS

MOVEMENTS

Go to the parable shelves and pick up the gold box with the white dot on it. Point to the dot, but you do not need to say anything about it.

Carry the box to the circle of children. Place it in the center of the circle. Touch it with pleasure and interest as you introduce the material to the children.

Move the parable box from the middle of the circle of children to your side. Remove the lid and lean it against the side of the box between the box and the children. This helps the children keep focused on what is already laid out and not worrying about what is coming next. It also keeps some of the mystery of the parable box in place.

Take out the underlay. Leave it crumpled in the middle of the circle for a few moments as you begin wondering what it could really be. As you continue wondering, smooth it out.

WORDS

Watch carefully where I go so you will always know where to find this lesson.

I wonder if there could be a parable inside this box? It is the color gold. There must be something important inside. Parables are very important, so maybe there is one inside this box.

Parables are very old, and this box looks old. Perhaps there is an old parable inside.

Did you know that parables were given to you before you were born? This box looks kind of like a present. Parables are presents, so maybe there is a parable inside this box.

Look at this lid. Sometimes parables have a lid on them, like a door that is shut. The lid keeps you from going inside the parable. I don't know why. This sometimes happens even if you are ready, so don't be discouraged. Keep coming back to the parable, and one day it will open up for you.

I have an idea. Let's look inside this box and see if there is a parable there.

Look at this. It is something. I don't know if it is a parable or not. Well, at least we can see that it is very white. Everywhere there is anything, it is white.

I wonder what this could really be? Yes, it looks like a snowball. It is cold. I wonder what else it could be? Could it be the moon, I wonder? I wonder what this could really be?

MOVEMENTS

When the wondering about the underlay is almost finished, take out the brown rectangular pieces one by one. You will not be able to tell which one you have because they are crumpled. Take them out at random. This helps your own sense of the parabolic. You will have a different configuration, something unsuspected, every time.

Put your finger on a corner of the figure and pull one of the sides from that point. Place your finger at the next corner and pull the next piece out to its length. Do this for each brown piece. This is a way to organize the setting up of the figures and it helps smooth them out. Place each brown piece at a different place on the underlay.

Place the merchant and the contents of his house in one of the brown rectangular figures farthest from you. Those contents include: bags of money, chair, a chest, candle, his bed, and other household or personal items. Place the seller and his table in the large brown figure that is closest to you. You will have three empty figures.

Take out the little gold box with the pearls inside. Let it sit for a moment and then open it with mystery. Silently place a pearl on the table in front of the seller. Put one pearl in two of the three empty rectangular figures.

WORDS

I wonder what this could be? It is brown, but what could it really be in the parable?

Hmmm. This is strange. I wonder if they fit together?

Oh, this helps.

Let's see if there is anything more inside the box to help us.

No. There is nothing else. All we can do now is begin.

MOVEMENTS   **WORDS**

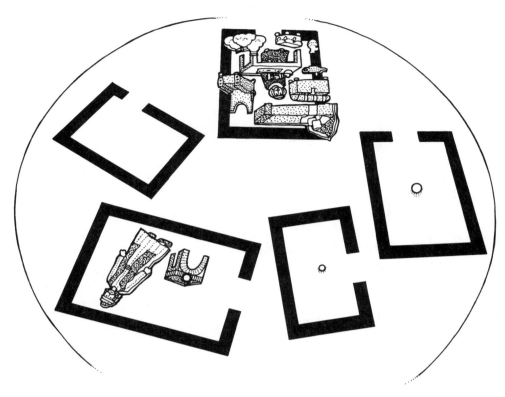

THE PARABLE OF THE GREAT PEARL (STORYTELLER'S PERSPECTIVE)

Sit back for a moment. Reflect silently on all that is laid out before you on the underlay. Wait until you are ready. If they need it, help the children get ready.

There was once someone who said such wonderful things and did such amazing things that people followed him. As they followed him, they heard him talking about a kingdom, but it was not the kingdom they lived in. It was not like any kingdom they had ever visited. It was not like any kingdom that they had ever even heard of.

They couldn't help it. They had to ask him what the kingdom of heaven was like. One time when they asked him, he said, "The kingdom of heaven is like when a person who buys and sells fine pearls, a merchant, goes to search for the great pearl."

Move the merchant out of his home's doorway and let him stop briefly at each of the other places (the brown outline shapes). Pick up the pearl when there is one there and hold it up close to your own eyes (for the merchant) and inspect it. Put it back and

MOVEMENTS

shake your head. It is not the great one. Finally, the merchant comes to the place where the seller is sitting behind a table. On the table is the great pearl. Pick it up and nod your head yes.

The merchant leaves the pearl on the table of the seller. He goes to his home and brings the bags of money.

He goes back and returns with the chest. He brings the chair, the vase, the candle...everything but his bed. Finally, he goes to get the last piece inside the house, which is his bed. He then returns to his house, folds it up and places it inside of the seller's house.

The merchant then goes back to where his house once was. Leave him there with the pearl, sitting right in the middle of his former home. Place the pearl at the center of the merchant.

There is, of course, silence during the movements of the merchant. Don't hurry. Acknowledge the questions of the children as well as their exclamations. Don't stop until you finish the sentence with the phrase "everything for the great pearl."

Sit back and rest for a moment before you begin the wondering. Prepare for your own wonder. It has to come from within you to be real.

WORDS

⇒ "When he found the great pearl, he went..."

⇒ "...and exchanged..."

⇒ "...everything for the great pearl."

⇒ I wonder if the person was happy with the great pearl?

I wonder what the merchant is going to do now?

I wonder why the seller was willing to give up something so precious?

I wonder if the seller was happy with all of his things?

I wonder if the seller has a name?

MOVEMENTS

WORDS

I wonder if the merchant has a name?

Now, I wonder what the great pearl could really be?

I wonder what could be so precious that a person would exchange everything for it?

I wonder if you have ever come close to the great pearl?

I wonder where this whole place could really be?

When the wondering concludes, put the pieces of the parable back carefully into the box. Don't hurry. Name each one as you put it away.

Here is the great pearl.
Here are two other pearls.
Here are all the merchant's new things.
Here are the places.
Here is the seller, and here is the merchant.

Return the parable box to the shelves and go back carefully to the circle. Sit down to help the children decide what work they are going to get out.

LESSON 10
PARABLE OF THE SOWER

LESSON NOTES
FOCUS: THE SOWER AND THE SEED (MATTHEW 13:1-9)
● PARABLE

● CORE PRESENTATION

THE MATERIAL
● LOCATION: PARABLE SHELVES

● PIECES: PARABLE BOX WITH LIGHT BROWN DOT, GOLD BOX OF BIRDS, 3
EARTH IMAGES (ROCKY SOIL, THORNS, GOOD EARTH), 3 BAGS OF GRAIN, 1
SOWER

● UNDERLAY: LIGHT BROWN

BACKGROUND
This parable is found in all three synoptic gospels and in the Gospel of Thomas (Mark 4:1–9; Matthew 13:1–9; Luke 8:4–8; Gospel of Thomas 9). The parable, which describes Jesus' promise of abundant harvest, is followed by an allegory that expresses the concerns of the first century Church.

NOTES ON THE MATERIAL
Find the material in a gold parable box with a light brown dot, located on the top shelf of one of the parable shelves. The underlay is a long strip of brown. There are three individual pieces with images representing the rocky soil, the thorns and the good earth. As you tell the parable, lay out the matching image for the kind of soil being described.

Three bags of grain, in increasing sizes, represent the harvests of thirty, sixty and one hundred measures. There is also a little gold box full of birds and the figure of the sower.

SPECIAL NOTES

Storytelling Tip: You'll find the introductions to each parable very similar. You need not repeat the words exactly the same each time, but do try to make your introductions similar. This repetition serves in the same way as the phrase "once upon a time" in many stories. Familiar words signal something out of the ordinary is about to happen.

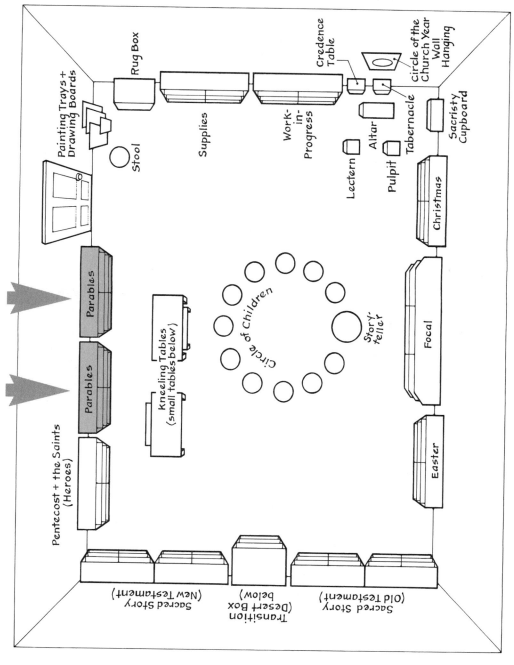

WHERE TO FIND MATERIALS

MOVEMENTS

Go to the parable shelves and pick up the parable box. Point to the light brown dot on the box that identifies it. Bring the parable box to the circle of children.

Sit back and reflect for a moment about what might be inside. This is not a hypothetical exercise on the part of the storyteller. You have no guarantee that what you take out will be a parable. As you say to the children, parables can be easily broken when people are not ready. Even if you are ready, there are days when you will not find the presentation to be a parable.

After using some or all these introductions, sit back a moment and reflect again on whether there is a parable inside the box. After a moment or two, you seem to have an idea.

Move the parable box from in front of you to your side. Remove the lid and lean it up against the box on the side where the children are sitting in the circle. This will help them keep focused on what is being presented rather than what is to come out of the box, and it helps keep the box more mysterious.

Take out the underlay. Leave it in a crumpled heap in the middle of the circle. As you talk about it, begin to smooth it out.

WORDS

⟹ Watch where I go to get this material.

⟹ Look, the box is the color gold. There may be a parable inside because parables are as valuable, or even more valuable, than gold.

The box also looks like a present. Parables are presents. They were given to you before you were born. They are yours, even if you don't know what they are.

This box looks old, and parables are old. Maybe there really is one inside.

Do you see the lid? It is like a closed door. Sometimes parables seem closed to us, even if we are ready to enter them. You need to keep coming back for them, and one day they will open.

⟹ I know what let's do. Let's look inside and see if there is a parable there.

⟹ I wonder what this could really be? It doesn't look like much now. Hmmm. It is certainly brown. It is all brown. Everywhere there is anything, there is brown.

Let's see if there is anything else in the box that can help us get the parable ready.

MOVEMENTS	WORDS
	There are many things here to help us tell the parable, but nothing else to help us get ready. All we can do then is begin.
	There was once someone who did such amazing things and said such wonderful things that people followed him. As they followed him, they heard him speaking about a kingdom. The kingdom was not like the one they were in. It was not like one that anyone had ever visited. It was not like any kingdom anyone had even heard about. So they had to ask him, "What is the kingdom of heaven like?"
Take the sower out of the box and place him on the underlay at your right facing toward the children.	One day when they asked him that, he said, "The kingdom of heaven is like when a sower, someone who scatters seeds, goes out and scatters seeds along the path."
Move the sower along the brown strip, scooping seeds from his basket with your hand, and sowing them along the underlay from your right to left. The sower stops.	
Take the gold box full of little birds from the parable box. Place it on the underlay between you and the "path." Remove the lid carefully.	"As the sower sowed seeds along the path, the birds of the air came..."
Take out the birds one by one and place them along the underlay (farthest from you) from your right to left. These are the birds who have come to eat the seeds.	"...and ate the seeds."
Take out the figure for the rocky ground and place it to your left of the birds that you lined up along the underlay farthest from you. Move the sower along that piece, scattering seeds from the bowl among the stones.	"The sower also sowed seeds among the stones."
The pushing down of the roots can be expressed with your hands by opening them and trying to push your fingers down among the stones.	"When the seeds tried to put their little roots down among the stones they could not push their way into the ground."
	"When the sun came out it scorched the seeds and they died."

MOVEMENTS	WORDS
Place the figure of the thorns to your left of the stones. Move the sower along the thorns, sowing as he goes.	"The sower also sowed seeds among the thorns."
The choking can be expressed by your hands. Clench both fists and twist them.	"When the seeds tried to push their little roots down among the thorns, they could push them part way in, but the thorns choked them, and they died."
Place the figure of the good earth to your left of the thorns. Move the sower along the good earth and scatter seeds with your hand, scooping seeds from the bowl the sower carries.	"The sower also sowed seeds in the good earth."
Use your fingers again to show the roots going down into the earth.	"When the seeds pushed their little roots down into the good earth, they could go all the way in. They grew and grew."
Move your flat hand across the top of the figure showing the good earth, to show the cutting off of the ripe grain during the harvest.	"When they were all grown up, they were ripe for the harvest. Then they were cut off and gathered up."
Take out of the parable box the figures for the thirty, sixty and one hundred bushels and place them from your right to your left in ascending order along the underlay farthest away from you. "Fill them" by scooping up the harvest with your hand and "pouring" it into the containers, being sure the picture side is toward the children.	"The harvest was thirty, sixty and one hundred bushels."
Pause for a moment after placing the containers of the harvest. Prepare yourself for the wondering. When you and the children are ready, begin.	
Move the sower to the middle.	Now, I wonder if the person had a name?
	I wonder who the person could really be?
	I wonder if the person was happy when the birds came and ate the seeds?

MOVEMENTS   ## WORDS

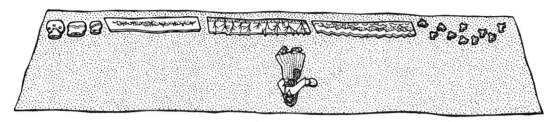

THE PARABLE OF THE SOWER (STORYTELLER'S PERSPECTIVE)

I wonder if the birds were happy when they saw the sower?

I wonder if the birds have names?

Move the sower from your right to left as you wonder.

I wonder what the person was doing when the little seeds could not get their roots in among the stones?

I wonder what the person was doing when the little seeds were choked by the thorns?

I wonder what the person was doing when the little seeds were growing in the good earth?

I wonder what the harvest could really be?

Move the thorn figure above the stone figure and then put the good earth above the thorns. Then move the thirty bushels to the left of the stones, the sixty bushels to the left of the thorns, and the one hundred bushels to the left of the good earth.

Was it like this?

Put the thirty bushels by the good earth and the sixty by the stones and the one hundred by the thorns. Continue moving the harvest baskets until all possible combinations are completed.

Or could it really be like this?

Move everything back to its place. Then move the harvest bags to the middle between you and the soil strips. Touch each bag as you wonder how the harvest was used.

I wonder what the sower used for seed?

I wonder what the sower sold?

I wonder what the sower kept for food?

MOVEMENTS

When the wondering winds down, begin to put all of the pieces of the parable carefully back in the parable box. Name the things as they are put away. Ask the children to begin thinking about what work they are going to get out during the response time.

When all is put away, replace the parable box on the shelf. Return to the circle of children and help them decide what work they would like to get out.

WORDS

I wonder if the sower was surprised at the harvest?

I wonder what part surprised the sower most?

➡ Here are the birds.
Etc.

PARABLE OF THE LEAVEN

LESSON NOTES

FOCUS: THE WOMAN AND THE LEAVEN (MATTHEW 13:33; LUKE 13:20-21)

- ● PARABLE
- ● CORE PRESENTATION

THE MATERIAL

- ● LOCATION: PARABLE SHELVES
- ● PIECES: PARABLE BOX WITH TAN DOT; BOX CONTAINING LOAF OF BREAD (1 FLAT PIECE AND 1 RISEN PIECE) AND 3 BOWLS OF FLOUR; BOX WITH TRIAN-GULAR GOLD LEAVEN
- ● UNDERLAY: TAN

BACKGROUND

The Parable of the Leaven is found in Matthew 13:33 and Luke 13:20–21. Many years ago, a little girl about five-years-old discovered what many people miss today about this parable. When commenting on her expressive art, she said, "The lady is Moses and the bread is not *matzo*." *Matzo*, the bread for the Jewish Passover, has no leaven in it.

In modern English, the term "leaven" has a positive connotation, but in ancient liter-ature, except for Jesus' parable, the connotation was universally negative. It was a sign of moral corruption, because fermentation is a process of putrefaction in the mass of dough. Leaven was made by storing a piece of bread in a dark, damp place until mold formed.

The children do not know about this ancient view of leavening, so the parable will define its own terms for them as it unfolds.

NOTES ON THE MATERIAL

Find the material in a gold parable box with a tan dot, located on the top shelf of one of the parable shelves. The underlay is tan, in the shape of a loaf of bread that has risen.

The loaf of bread in the parable comes in pieces. First, there is a wide, flat piece with a tall, rounded shape above it. This is so the flat piece can be laid down first, the leaven, hidden just above it, and then the rounded piece placed over the leaven when the loaf is leavened. The underlay, then, suggests the leaven and unleavened loaves.

There are three bowls with flour in them. The woman's figure is extended from her shape to a table on which to put the other things. The leaven is a little golden triangle.

SPECIAL NOTES

Storytelling Tip: Please put the leaven in its own mysterious little box. The rest of the parable objects—flat bread, risen bread and the three bowls with flour—can be put together in another little box, placed within the gold parable box that also holds the underlay.

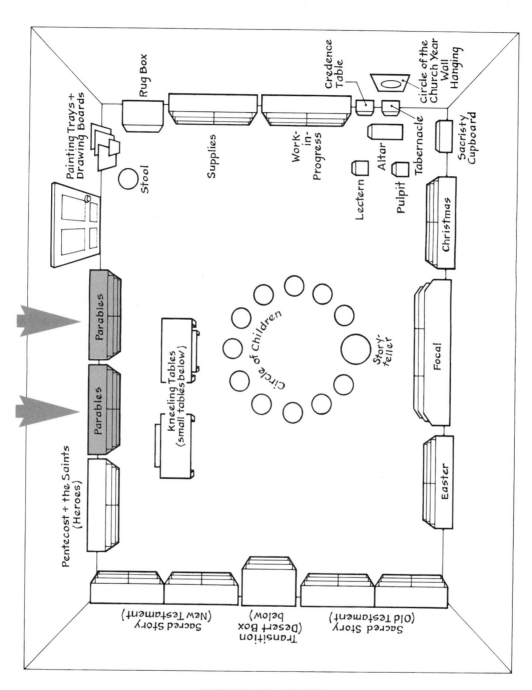

WHERE TO FIND MATERIALS

MOVEMENTS

WORDS

You go first to the parable shelves and pick up the box with the small tan circle on it. Tan is also the color of this parable's underlay. You don't need to say anything. Point to the small circle.

Bring the parable to the circle of children and place it in the middle to wonder about the box and its content.

▶ Now, let's see. The box is the color gold. Something valuable must be inside. Parables are very valuable, even more important than gold, so maybe there is a parable inside.

The box looks kind of like a present. Parables are like presents. They were given to you even before you were born. They are yours. You don't need to take them. They are already yours even if you do not know what they are.

The box has a lid. It stops us. You see, sometimes, even if we are really ready, it is hard to go inside a parable. They are just like that. I don't know why. Don't be discouraged if you can't find your way in. Keep coming back, and one day the parable will open up for you.

I have an idea. Let's see what is inside the box. Maybe there is a parable inside.

Move the box to your side. Take off the lid and leave it tipped against the side of the box next to the circle.

Take out the underlay. Leave it crumpled up in the middle of the circle for a moment, and then begin to smooth it out.

▶ I wonder what this could be? Hmm. I can't tell. It is a kind of brown, though. It is sort of yellow and brown, a kind of tan.

How strange. I wonder what it could really be?

Let's see if there is anything else in the box to help us get ready for the parable.

Look carefully into the box. There is nothing there to help get ready. The pieces left all have to do with the telling of the parable.

▶ Oh, no, I have some bad news! There is nothing else. All we can do is just begin.

There was once someone who said such amazing things and did such wonderful things that people followed him. As they followed him, they heard him talking about a kingdom, but it was not like the kingdom they lived in. It was not like any kingdom anyone had ever visited. It was not even like any kingdom anyone had ever heard of. They couldn't help it. They had to ask him what the kingdom of heaven was like.

MOVEMENTS

You take out the woman-table figure and place it in the middle of the underlay. Turn it so she is right-side up for most of the children in the circle. She faces away from you.

Place the three containers of flour on the table. Line them up, because they will be covered by the flat bread representation.

Place the figure representing the flat bread over the three containers for the flour, making a stirring movement with your finger.

The leaven is a small gold triangle. Place it above—not covering—the flat bread and the three measures.

WORDS

One time when they asked him this, he said "The kingdom of heaven is like a woman..."

"...who took three measures of flour, which is a lot..."

"...and mixed them together."

"She hid the leaven in the mixture which swelled up and was leavened all over."

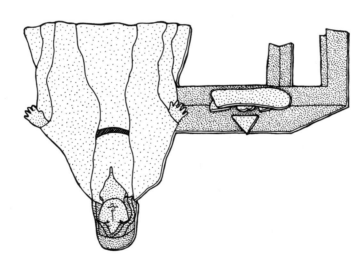

THE LEAVEN AND THE FLAT BREAD (STORYTELLER'S PERSPECTIVE)

Place the bigger rounded figure of the bread above (not on top of) the flat one and on top of the leaven so the risen loaf and the flat bread are one.

"It got big and puffy like the bread you buy in the store."

MOVEMENTS   **WORDS**

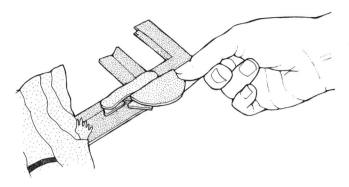

CREATING THE RISEN LOAF (STORYTELLER'S PERSPECTIVE)

Pause. Lean back. Begin the wondering.

Now, I wonder if the woman has a name? I wonder who she could really be?

I wonder if the woman was happy?

I wonder what the bread could really be?

I wonder what the leaven is, really, in the parable and in life?

I wonder if you could take the bread that was leavened all over and put it back like it was before the woman hid the leaven in it?

I wonder if you have ever come close to a place where this happens? I mean really, not just in the parable or making bread?

Lean back and reflect for a moment on all of these wonderings. You then begin to put things away, slowly and carefully, one at a time.

While I am putting everything away, please begin to think about what work you are going to get out.

Watch now, where I go to put this parable away, so you will always know where to find it.

LESSON 12

PARABLE OF THE MUSTARD SEED

LESSON NOTES

FOCUS: THE MUSTARD SEED AND SHRUB (MATTHEW 24:32; MARK 4:30-32; LUKE 13:18-19)

- PARABLE
- CORE PRESENTATION

THE MATERIAL

- LOCATION: PARABLE SHELVES
- PIECES: PARABLE BOX WITH YELLOW DOT, GREEN FELT SHRUB (OR TREE), GOLD BOX WITH BIRDS AND NESTS, FIGURE OF A PERSON
- UNDERLAY: YELLOW

BACKGROUND

This parable is found in all three synoptic gospels and in Thomas (Matthew 24:32; Mark 4:30–32; Luke 13:18–19; Gospel of Thomas 20). The mustard in the parable is not the domestic mustard we use for flavoring. The mustard of the eastern world grew and spread quickly. Farmers did not like it because it could take over a field and ruin its useful production of grain. It is a shrub and not a tree. These historical matters are not interesting to children, but they are mentioned to invite the reader to discover more about this parable as an adult.

NOTES ON THE MATERIAL

Find the material in a gold parable box with a yellow dot, located on the top shelf of one of the parable shelves. The underlay is yellow and shaped with the top a bit wider than the bottom. The sides are curved like a seed. The shape suggests a seed and more. There is a green shrub or tree made of felt to be unrolled. Birds and nests are kept in a separate small gold box with a lid. Finally, there is the figure of a person who puts the tiny seed in the ground.

SPECIAL NOTES

Tip: Why tell parables? In parables, we enter with wonder to live the question. Parables question our everyday view of life. They wake us up to see in life what we have not seen before. Parables question the status quo, the order imposed by tradition, power or class. That is why Jesus' parables often got him into trouble, and why Christians ever since have sometimes redefined parables in ways that comfort us *only* rather than challenge us by disrupting our comfortable worldviews.

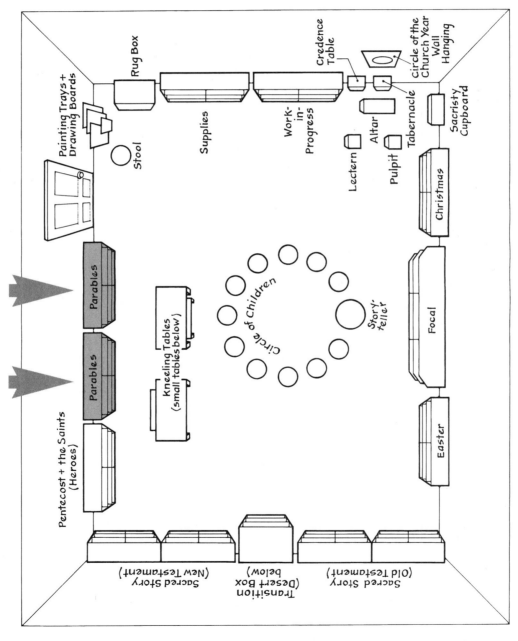

WHERE TO FIND MATERIALS

MOVEMENTS	WORDS
Go to the parable shelf and pick up the parable box with the yellow dot on it. Point to the dot, but do not say anything to the children. Bring the parable box to the circle of children and place it in the middle. Sit down and become comfortable.	Watch where I go to get this material.
As you speak, pick up the box and look at it more closely.	This box looks old. Parables are old. I wonder if there is a parable inside?
Trace the outline of the box as you speak about its color and value.	The box is the color gold. Parables are valuable, maybe even more valuable than gold.
Knock on the lid, like knocking on a door, when you note the difficulty of entering parables at times.	Look, the box has a lid. I know, boxes have lids, but so do parables. Sometimes, even if you are ready, you cannot enter the parable. The lid is like a door. Sometimes it is closed. If that happens don't be discouraged. Come back to the parable again and again. One day it will open for you.
Hold the box out like a present.	The box looks like a present. Parables are presents. They were given to you before you were born. Even if you do not know what a parable is, it has still been given to you.
When several or all of the introduction sentences are finished, sit for a moment. Let your authentic interest and love of parables be apparent.	I know what let's do. Let's look inside to see if there really is a parable there. I know they are easy to break, so let's be careful.
Move the box from in front of you to your side. Remove the lid and lean it on the box so the children will not be distracted by looking inside. This also helps maintain a sense of mystery.	
Take out the underlay and leave it for a moment crumpled in front of you. Then begin to smooth it out as you talk.	I wonder what this could be? I wonder if it could be a parable? It is certainly yellow.
Hold your hand a few inches above the underlay. Push your hand down into the "color" that is there. Imply that the "yellow" has substance to it beyond the cloth. Invite the children to play with the idea of what the underlay could be.	There is nothing else here but yellow. I wonder what this could really be? Yes, I know it does look like a lemon.

I know, it could be the sun. I wonder what else it could really be? |

MOVEMENTS

Take out the rolled up green felt tree and hide it inside your closed hand. While you are hiding it, keep eye contact with the children so they will look at you rather than at the material.

Look carefully into the box. There is nothing there to help get ready. The pieces left all have to do with the telling of the parable.

Take the person figure from the parable box. Place it at the edge of the underlay farthest from you, facing the children. The shrub will be planted there and grow "up" (from the children's perspective) toward you.

Hold up your closed hand that contains the "tree" and cover it with your other hand. Extend the first finger of the closed hand to show that you cannot see the seed. This kind of mustard seed comes in a pod and the individual seeds are like dust. You really could not see it.

Put your finger down into the underlay to plant the seed close to the farthest edge.

WORDS

A lemon drop? I wonder.

Let's see if there is anything else in here that can help us get ready.

Oh no, there isn't anything else! All we can do is begin.

There was once someone who said such wonderful things and did such amazing things that people followed him. As they followed him, they heard him speaking about a kingdom, but it was not like the kingdom they lived in. It was not like any kingdom they had ever visited. It was not even like any kingdom anyone had ever heard of.

They couldn't help it. They had to ask him. What is the kingdom of heaven like? One time when they asked him that he said, "The kingdom of heaven is like when a person..."

"...took the tiniest of all the seeds, a grain of mustard seed, a seed so small that if I had one on my finger you would not be able to see it."

"The person put the tiny seed in the ground, and it began..."

MOVEMENTS

Inside your closed hand is the felt tree, so when you say "grow" you can begin to unroll it. Unroll it all the way to its top and then begin to extend the branches that were folded first, the last time you put the parable away.

Take the small gold box out of the parable box. Set it down on the underlay. Do not hurry. Remove the lid. Take a few of the birds out of the box, one at a time. Place them flying toward the tree.

Take a few other birds from the box, one at a time, and place them around the tree. Take a few nests from the box, and place them in the branches of the tree.

WORDS

"...to grow."

"The shrub grew up so big it was like a little tree, and the birds of the air came..."

"...and they made their nests there."

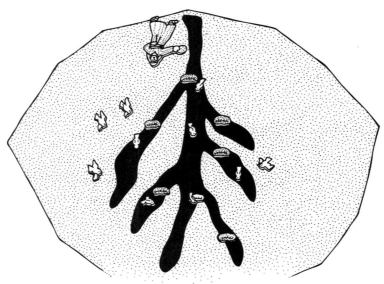

THE PARABLE OF THE MUSTARD SEED (STORYTELLER'S PERSPECTIVE)

Sit back and enjoy the birds and the tree. If the children are well settled, you might pass around the box of birds and nests and invite the children to put birds and nests in places that are just right for them.

MOVEMENTS

When you are finished with the birds and nests, it is time to begin the wondering.

WORDS

Now I wonder if the person who put the tiny seed in the ground has a name?

I wonder if the person was happy to see the birds coming?

I wonder what the person was doing while the shrub was growing?

I wonder if the person could take the shrub like a tree and push it all back down inside the seed?

I wonder if the seed was happy while it was growing?

I wonder where the seed was when it stopped growing?

I wonder if the birds have names?

I wonder if they were happy to find the tree?

I wonder what the tree could really be?

I wonder if you have ever come close to this kind of tree?

I wonder what the nests could really be?

I wonder where this whole place could really be?

When the wondering draws to a close, begin to place the birds and nests back into the little box first, and then put the rest of the objects into the parable box itself. While you are putting things away, you might name the things again. This also is a good time to ask the children to begin to think about what work they will get out during the response time. The underlay goes in last.

Take the parable box back to the parable shelves, return to the circle and begin to help the children decide what work they will get out.

ENRICHMENT LESSON

PARABLE OF PARABLES

LESSON NOTES

FOCUS: A PARABLE ABOUT PARABLES

● PARABLE

● ENRICHMENT PRESENTATION

THE MATERIAL

● LOCATION: PARABLE SHELVES

● PIECES: TRAY OR BASKET HOLDING A SET OF NESTING BOXES IN ASSORTED COLORS

● UNDERLAY: NONE (USE RUG)

BACKGROUND

Sometimes children will ask, "What's really inside a parable?" You have introduced this idea with every parable presentation, so it is exciting when the question is finally raised. This is the moment you have been waiting for. Now you can say, "We have a parable about that!"

NOTES ON THE MATERIAL

Find the material for this lesson on the second shelf of one of the parable shelves. (The top shelves hold the six guiding parables.) Use a rug, not an underlay, so you don't give away the number of boxes within boxes. The material is not in a gold box, because this is not a parable that Jesus told. Instead, the materials are kept on a tray or in a basket.

The material is a set of what are sometimes called Chinese boxes or nested boxes. They are boxes of assorted colors that fit inside one another. The present set of ten boxes that Jerome uses range from about 5"-square for the largest box to about 1"-square for the smallest box.

SPECIAL NOTES

Tip: Godly Play parables include six guiding parables as well as parables *about* parables. Older children who are thoroughly familiar with the guiding parables are ready for this enrichment lesson, even if they haven't yet asked, "What's really inside a parable?" As with any presentation, this lesson can be given to an individual child, to a small group or to the whole class.

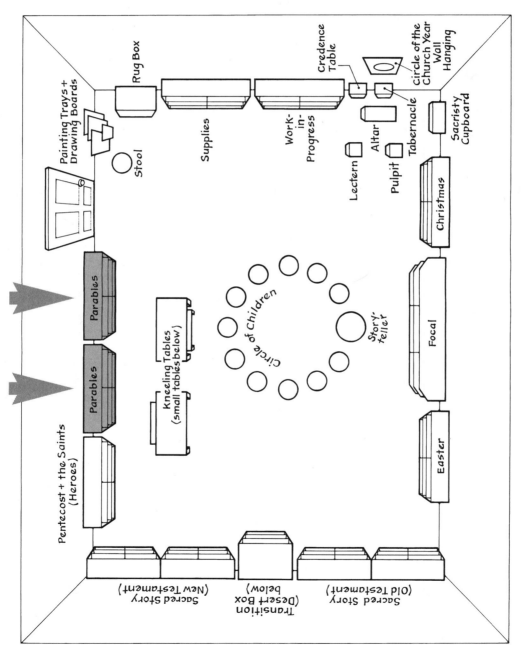

WHERE TO FIND MATERIALS

MOVEMENTS	WORDS
Go to the rug box and get a rug. Spread it out in the middle of the circle of children. Go to the parable shelves and get the tray or basket with the Parable of Parables in it. Return to the circle and place the basket or tray beside you. Leave the box at your side for a few moments.	Watch where I go so you will know where to find this lesson.
Place the box in the center of the rug.	Sometimes people wonder what is really inside a parable. Here is a parable that shows you. See, this is not a parable of Jesus. It is not gold like the other parables. This is a different kind of parable, so it is smaller and a different color. I wonder what really is inside a parable. All we have to do is take off the lid to find out. Be careful! You need to be really ready to do this.
Slowly remove the lid from the outer box of the nested boxes. Look shocked to find another box inside. Place the empty box on the rug at your right. A line of empty boxes will develop from your right to your left.	What is this? Is it a box inside a box? Oh, no! It's a parable inside a parable, like a box is inside a box. That is very interesting, but what we really want to know is what is inside a parable. Let's look in this one to find out.
Slowly remove the next box's lid. Again, look shocked. Place this second box to your left of the first box.	What is this? Another box inside of a box? Okay. I understand. A parable is inside a parable, like a box is inside a box. I get it. We don't need any more boxes inside of boxes. Let's see now what is really inside a parable.
Slowly, remove the next box's lid. Again, look shocked.	Okay. So there are boxes inside of boxes, like parables are inside of parables. Look here's another one. Here's another one.
Go through several boxes rather quickly and then pause again. Slowly remove the box's lid and again appear to be shocked. Continue.	Now, this must be the last one. People don't make boxes smaller than this.
Open the next box. Respond with surprise. There is another box inside of this one.	

MOVEMENTS

WORDS

Here's a gold one. This must be the one we have been waiting for. This must be the last one. Now, we can see what is really inside of a parable.

Finally, you will come to the last box. Open it carefully. Lean over and look inside. Lean closer. Put your thumb and first or second finger together to take the "inside" of the parable out.

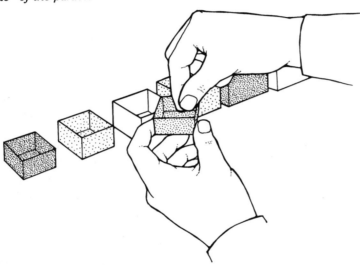

TAKING OUT THE "INSIDE" OF THE PARABLE (STORYTELLER'S PERSPECTIVE)

Hold up the "inside," an imaginary final box or presence. Place it in the air just about two feet in front of your eyes. Let your fingers go as it is sitting there in the air. (There is nothing to be seen, but you treat it as if it were tangible.) Sit for a moment and continue to look at the unseen "inside." Do not let any movement or sounds from the children disturb you as you continue to gaze at it.

It's hard to see, isn't it. That is why people who loved parables very much put it in a box, so they can find it and even take it with them.

MOVEMENTS

Use your thumb and finger again to take hold of the "inside" of the parable as it sits there in the air. Place it carefully in the smallest box again. Put the lid back on.

If the children challenge this invisible "inside" of a parable, remind them that Jesus spoke the parables. Words that are written down are easy to see, but words that are spoken are not. You might ask, "Can you see the words I am saying right now?"

Place the first box in the second box and place the lid on the second box. Put it back in the line of boxes in the middle of the rug, sit back and reflect on what has happened for a moment before you proceed.

Place the two nested boxes in the next larger box and put the lid on it. Along about this time you will need to speed up the process and do several boxes at once.

You have now placed the nested boxes in the next to last box. The last box will be the parents' box.

WORDS

⟹ They didn't want to lose the parable. It was too precious.

⟹ The next people who came along also loved parables very much, but the parable box the first people made wasn't quite right for them, so they made their own.

The next people who came along also loved parables very much, but the box the other people made didn't agree with them very well. They wanted one that was just right for them, so they made their own.

⟹ People kept doing this. Someone would come along and find the parable box someone else made and like it, but it wasn't just right for the new person, so one that was just right had to be made. When the next people came along and did the same thing. This went on for hundreds of years.

Even after a thousand years this was still going on. Then, about the time America was discovered, it was still happening.

Finally, your grandmothers and grandfathers, who loved parables very much, found the parable box the people who came before them had made. They liked it, but it was not just right for them, so they made their own.

⟹ Finally, we come to the time of your mothers and fathers. They love parables very much too, but the box that their mothers and fathers made was not quite right for them. They had to make their very own.

MOVEMENTS

Place the nested boxes in the last (and largest) box and put the lid on it. The whole set of nesting boxes is now sitting in the middle of the rug. Stop a moment and silently reflect on what has happened.

When the wondering about this is drawing to a close, you might begin other wonderings.

When the wondering is finished, put the nest of boxes back in the basket or on the tray. Replace the tray or basket on the parable shelves. Roll up the rug and replace it in the rug box. Return to the circle and begin to help the children decide what work they will get out.

WORDS

I wonder who is going to make the next parable box?

I wonder what the box could really be?

I wonder what the whole line of boxes makes?

I wonder what kind of box is just right for you?

I wonder if you have ever come close to the inside of a parable?

ENRICHMENT LESSON
PARABLE OF THE DEEP WELL

LESSON NOTES
FOCUS: A RABBINICAL PARABLE ABOUT PARABLES

- PARABLE
- ENRICHMENT PRESENTATION

THE MATERIAL

- LOCATION: PARABLE SHELVES
- PIECES: PARABLE BOX WITH 1 WELL, 1 CONTAINER OF GOLDEN THREADS AND 1 BUCKET
- UNDERLAY: BROWN

BACKGROUND

From time to time children ask what parables really are. To help them find their own interpretation of what a parable is, another parable can be proposed. You might say, "We have a parable about that," and present this parable to the child. You also might want to present it to the group as well.

This parable has its roots in the traditions of the rabbis. You can find more information by looking up "Midrash Rabbah on the Song of Songs 1.1.8." as quoted in *Hear Then the Parable*, by Bernard Brandon Scott (Minneapolis: Fortress Press, 1991) or consult the great translation of the *Midrash Rabbah* by H. Freedman and Maurice Simon (London: Soncino Press, 1999).

NOTES ON THE MATERIAL

Since this parable is not a parable of Jesus, you will find it in a plain wooden box on the second shelf of one of the parables shelves. In the box is an underlay of brown felt in an irregular shape.

Inside the box is also a round "well," about the same size as the largest nesting box used for the Parable of Parables. In a clear container are many golden "threads," lengths of gold cord about 4"-5". (If they are shorter they will be hard to tie together.) You will also find a small bucket, small enough to be able to be "lowered into the well."

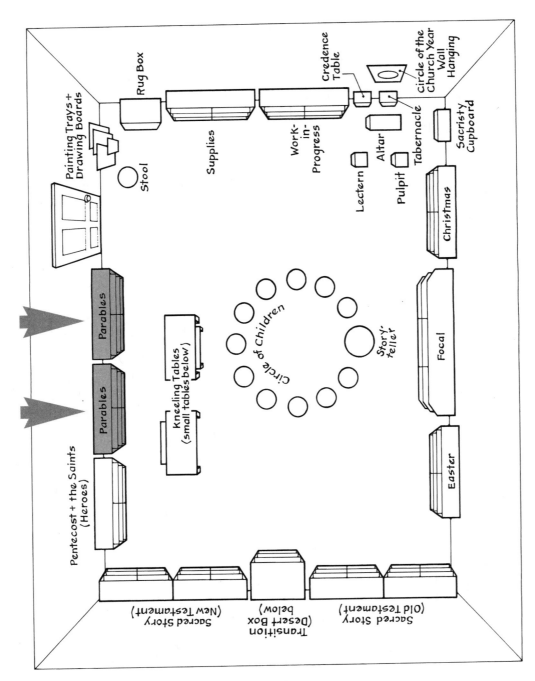

WHERE TO FIND MATERIALS

MOVEMENTS

Go to the parable shelves and get the plain wooden box. It is on the second shelf. The original six gold parable boxes (the parables of Jesus) are on the top shelves. Bring the box back to the circle and place it before you in the middle of the circle.

Sit back and look at it for a moment.

Slide the box beside you. Open the lid and take out the underlay. Place the underlay in front of you so that it is rather crumpled up.

Smooth out the underlay. Take your time.

Pull out the well, but do not name it.

Wait. Hold it in your hands. Be at ease with silence if there is any. See if the children will help you build the metaphor.

Place the "well" in the middle of the underlay.

Place the little bucket anywhere on the underlay.

Bring out the gold threads, but do not name them.

Scatter the golden threads (cord pieces) across the underlay. Sit back and reflect on what is there.

WORDS

Watch carefully where I go so you will always know where to find this lesson.

This is a parable, but it is not one of the parables of Jesus. We keep them in gold boxes. This box is plain wood. Many of you have asked what a parable really is. This is a parable about that, among other things.

Hmm, I wonder what this could really be? It is rather brown, but it has no real shape.

I wonder what could be so brown? There is no green or blue here at all. Hmm.

Let's see if there is anything else in here that can help us get ready.

Oh, look. Here is...something.

Hmm.

Let's see if there is anything else. Oh, look.

Here's more. I don't know what they are, but there are lots of them.

MOVEMENTS	WORDS

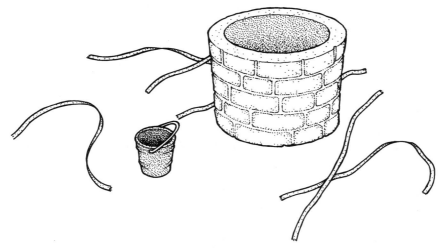

THE PARABLE OF THE DEEP WELL (STORYTELLER'S PERSPECTIVE)

Sweep your hand across the brown underlay.	There was once a great desert.
	In the middle of the desert was a deep well. It was so deep that people could no longer reach the water to drink.
Lean out over the well and look down into it. Touch your face as if you had just felt the refreshing coolness. Lean back and ponder this.	They could not even see the water in the well. Sometimes you could feel the damp coolness rising from the well, but there was no way to get the refreshing liquid from its depths.
	People cannot live in the desert without water. It is hot and it is easy to get lost. The wind changes the shape of the sand. There is nothing green to give shade or for people to eat, so everyone hurries across the sand and dirt to get away from the danger.
	One day a person crossed the desert. When the person came to the well, the person took time. There was no hurry. The person looked at the well and the little golden strands in the desert.
Pick up the little bucket and look at it. Turn it around and then put it back away from the well.	The person picked up a rusty object, but no one could remember what it was for. It was like a big cup you could carry, but where would a person get any water?
Move your hand across the desert and "kick" at some of the strands with your fingers.	The person looked again and kicked the golden threads. They seemed out of place. What were they? Other people thought they were silly and went on their way. This person took time.

MOVEMENTS

Tie about six or seven of the threads together as you talk. You then tie the long strand to the handle of the bucket.

Hold up high the strand with the bucket attached and begin to "lower" the bucket into the well. Let the cord collapse and go into the well; the bucket cannot be seen since it is shorter than the side of the well.

Pour the "water" from the bucket into your hand and "taste" some. Pass the bucket around the circle. The children are invited by your gesture to also "taste" it.

Alternative ending: After tasting the refreshing water untie the golden strands and scatter them.

WORDS

The person went back to the big cup with the handle and then to the deep well. Then the person began to walk around picking up the golden threads and tying them together.

The person lowered the bucket into the well and drew forth the refreshing water. The person tasted the water and was changed. When the person went on the way, the bucket and the many strands tied together were left, so the next person could also taste the water.

Here, you can taste it too.

Now, I wonder what the water from the well could really be?

I wonder where the desert could really be?

I wonder if you have ever crossed that desert?

I wonder what the deep well could really be?

I wonder if you have ever come close to the golden threads?

I wonder what the golden threads could really be?

I wonder why the person stopped and wondered?

I wonder how to wonder?

I wonder why?

Now, what about this ending: When the person went on the way, the little golden strands were untied and scattered again, so the next person could figure this out too.

I wonder which one of the endings you like best?

I wonder which one is the most important?

I wonder what part of the parable is especially about you?

I wonder if there is any part of this parable we could leave out and still have all the parable we need?

ENRICHMENT LESSON

PARABLE SYNTHESIS 1
ALL THE PARABLES

LESSON NOTES

FOCUS: THE PARABLES AS TEXTS

- PARABLE
- ENRICHMENT PRESENTATION (SYNTHESIS)

THE MATERIAL

- LOCATION: PARABLE SHELVES
- PIECES: LARGE BASKET CONTAINING 40 GOLD PARABLE CARDS (RECTANGLES) AND 15 GOLD "I AM" CARDS (TRIANGLES); BIBLE
- UNDERLAY: NONE

BACKGROUND

This material introduces the children to the whole corpus of the parables. Of course, the children will work with individual parables, but playing with the whole set of parables makes possible a new image and discovery—another parable.

Scholars disagree on the number of parables in scripture, depending on how they define *parable.* The Godly Play set of parables primarily follows the definitions used in Bernard Brandon Scott's book *Hear Then the Parable* (Minneapolis: Fortress Press, 1991).

There are two differences between the Godly Play set and Scott's grouping. First, the Godly Play corpus omits two parables that Scott includes from the Gospel of Thomas (A Woman with a Jar and A Man Who Had Hidden Treasure). Second, the Godly Play corpus includes two parables that Scott excludes from his list (the two traditional parables of the Ten Virgins and the Wheat and the Tares); Scott considers these to be inauthentic (*Hear Then the Parables,* pp. 68–72).

The Godly Play corpus, then, has thirty-one different parables, but you will find more than thirty-one gold cards if you count them. This is because a few parables are so long that the story carries over onto another card and because repeated parables are included in this count.

Scott also divides the parables into three groups:
- Family, Village, City and Beyond
- Home and Farm
- Masters and Servants

All but one of the six Godly Play guiding parables come from the Home and Farm group. The exception is the Good Samaritan, which Scott calls "From Jerusalem to Jericho" and places in the group called Family, Village, City and Beyond.

The Gospel of John: Scott does not call anything from John's Gospel a parable. Sofia Cavalletti and others have named two texts in John parables. One text tells about sheep and shepherds, and the other text is about the true vine. If these are not parables, what are they? They are from a group of sayings that might be called Jesus' self-identity statements or the "I Am" statements.

Since there is no narrative in the "I Am" statements, they are not parables, and yet they are parabolic. What shall we do? The Godly Play material for the "I Am" statements is printed on triangular pieces of wood. Parable Synthesis 2 (pp. 139-147) focuses on the fifteen "I Am" statements found in John.

The "Gospel" of Thomas: The Gospel of Thomas lists only sayings of Jesus, with no accompanying narrative structure. The Gospel of Thomas is widely available, but you may choose not to mention it because it is not in our Bible. The only reason to include it is because it is referred to by most parable scholars today, who use it to help with parable interpretation. The children will not be surprised or disturbed later when they find Thomas being used widely as an aid to interpret Jesus' parables in the Bible.

NOTES ON THE MATERIAL

Find the material in a large basket placed on the lowest shelf of one of the parable shelves. The material is a complete set of Jesus' parables written on gold wooden rectangles (about 8.5" x 5.5") and a complete set of Jesus' "I Am" statements written on gold wooden triangles (about 8.5" on each side).

Here is a list of the scriptures found on the parable cards (citations shown in parentheses indicate where the parables are found in other gospels):
- Matthew 13:1-9 (Mark 4:1-9; Luke 8:4-8)
- Matthew 13:24-30
- Matthew 13:31-32 (Mark 4:30-32; Luke 13:18-19)
- Matthew 13:33 (Luke 13:20-21)
- Matthew 13:44
- Matthew 13:45-46
- Matthew 13:47
- Matthew 18:12-14 (Luke 15:1-7)
- Matthew 18:23-34
- Matthew 21:28-31a
- Matthew 21:33-46 (Mark 12:1-12; Luke 20:9-19)
- Matthew 24:32 (Mark 13:28; Luke 21:29-30)

- Matthew 24:45-51 (Luke 12:42-46)
- Matthew 25:1-13
- Mark 4:1-9 (Matthew 13:1-9; Luke 8:4-8)
- Mark 4:26-29
- Mark 4:30-32 (Matthew 13:31-32; Luke 13:18-19)
- Mark 12:1-12 (Matthew 21:33-46, Luke 20:9-19)
- Mark 13:28 (Matthew 24:32; Luke 21:29-30)
- Mark 13:34-36 (Luke 12:36-38)
- Luke 7:41-42
- Luke 8:4-8 (Matthew 13:1-9; Mark 4:1-9)
- Luke 10:30-35
- Luke 11:5-8
- Luke 12:16-20
- Luke 12:36-38 (Mark 13:34-36)
- Luke 12:42-46 (Matthew 24:45-51)
- Luke 13:6-9
- Luke 13:18-19 (Matthew 13:31-32; Mark 4:30-32)
- Luke 13:20-21 (Matthew 13:33)
- Luke 14:16-24 (Matthew 22:2-14)
- Luke 15:1-7 (Matthew 18:12-14)
- Luke 15:8-10
- Luke 15:11-32
- Luke 16:1-8a
- Luke 17:7-9
- Luke 18:2-5
- Luke 18:10-14a
- Luke 20:9-19 (Matthew 21:33-46; Mark 12:1-12)
- Luke 21:29-30 (Matthew 24:32; Mark 13:28)

Here is a list of the scriptures found on the "I Am" cards:

- John 10:7-9
- John 10:11
- John 13:19
- John 11:25-27
- John 15:1
- John 14:5
- John 9:37
- John 8:58
- John 6:35
- John 8:12
- John 6:20
- John 18:5
- John 8:23
- John 8:18
- John 4:26

The cards are mixed together in a large basket in the classroom, so that the first discovery children make is that there are different shapes in the basket. You also will need a Bible.

At the bottom of each parable card are citations that refer the children to Matthew, Mark and Luke. (The citations maintain this order of the synoptic gospels.) The citations help the children see at a glance how many times a parable appears in the gospels and where it can be found. For example, the Parable of the Good Samaritan appears in only one gospel (Luke 10:30–35), so the places for Matthew and Mark citations are left blank on that card.

The parable cards do not have names identifying the parables, because there are games that invite the children to play with naming parables. Also, once a parable is named, an interpretation already has been made.

On the bottom of each "I Am" triangle is a citation to refer children to where the statement can be found in John. The triangular shape of these cards suggests the Trinity. We do not say this to the children but allow the shape to keep suggesting this at some level until a child makes his or her own discovery that Jesus, as the second person of the Trinity, has told us directly (in a parabolic way) who he is.

SPECIAL NOTES

Tip: The parable synthesis lessons (pp. 132-152) shift from the teaching objects for the six guiding parables to the more abstract and text-linked cards. This material is for children about nine years old and older. Children need to be comfortable with reading to enjoy working with the parables as texts.

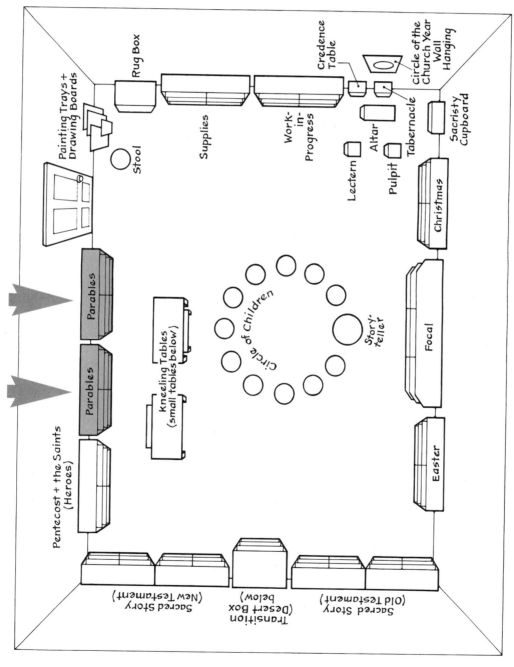

WHERE TO FIND MATERIALS

MOVEMENTS

You do not need an underlay or rug for this presentation. When you lay out the cards for all of the parables, they will cover an area larger than a rug.

Go to the parable shelves and pick up the large basket full of parable text cards and the "I Am" statements. Scatter the tiles on the floor.

Begin to sort through the pile with gratitude. Slowly separate the triangles and rectangles into two piles.

Read from a brief parable card picked at random, then read from a triangular card.

Pick two more and pair them side by side. Read them.

Show the children the citations on the rectangle cards and triangle cards.

Pick up the Bible which you placed beside you. (You also may want to have a Bible for each child or each two children.)

Read the card. Read from the Bible.

Show the children a card that has more than one citation.

As you say the word asterisk, *point to it on the card.*

Sit back and enjoy looking at all the parables scattered in the center of the circle.

WORDS

Look! Here are the parables.

There are so many. These words are the closest ones we have to what Jesus really said. You can almost hear his voice in these words.

Wait a minute. There are two different shapes here. What's going on? Let me read something from each shape.

Do you hear the difference? Listen again!

Some are parables. They have at least some story. The others tell when Jesus says who he is.

Look at the bottom of each card. Here are the names of the three gospels. Do you see the numbers following them?

Now, let's see how this works. Here is the Bible.

Here is a card that says *(read from the card).* Let's turn to that gospel and find the number. Listen.

They are the same. The numbers are called "citations." They tell you where to look in the Bible to find the parable.

Sometimes a parable is found in more than one place.

You can tell which version of the parable you have on the card by looking for the number with the asterisk beside it. That is the one you are reading. It is fun to see if parables are different when they are told in different gospels. That's the way stories are sometimes.

There are so many. It is wonderful.

The "I Am" statements. The parables.

MOVEMENTS

WORDS

Now I wonder what the parables could really be?

I wonder what the "I Am" statements could really be?

I wonder what all of the parables and the "I Am" statements make when you put them all together.

Put all the cards back into the large basket. When it is full, stand up and carry it carefully with two hands back to the parable shelves.

Return to the circle and, using both hands, carefully pick up the Bible and carry it to the part of the room where you keep your Bible.

Return to the circle again and sit. Look around the circle.

It is time to get out your work. Good. That's the way. You need to be ready.

You might want to work with the parables or you might want to make something about how you feel about all of the parables when they are together. You may have other projects you want to work on or other materials you want to wonder about.

Be thinking about what you are going to do as I go around the circle.

Appendix for the Gospel of Thomas: What do you say if an older child asks about the Gospel of Thomas?

The Gospel of Thomas is not one of the official stories of Jesus picked by the early Church to include in the Bible. It is not even a story! It is a list of 114 of Jesus' sayings. It is interesting, be-cause thirteen of the 114 sayings are like ones in the Bible.

Continue with this discussion as long as the children are interested.

The Gospel of Thomas is part of a library of fifty-two pieces (trac-tates) rolled into twelve books plus one piece from a thirteenth roll.

The whole library was found in 1945 at a place in Egypt called Nag Hammadi. It was someone's—or some group's—collection of what they thought were important texts about religion. It was copied from Greek into Coptic (Egyptian written with the Greek alphabet) about 200 c.e., and it was buried about 200 years later (400 c.e.). This is older than any of the more complete manu-scripts we have of the biblical gospels.

MOVEMENTS

WORDS

The first complete copy of the Greek New Testament known to us was copied in the fourth century C.E., so the manuscript of the Gospel of Thomas was copied about 200 years earlier. The gospels of the Bible, however, were written much earlier, in the first century of our era.

PARABLE SYNTHESIS 2 THE "I AM" STATEMENTS

LESSON NOTES

FOCUS: THE "I AM" STATEMENTS IN THE GOSPEL OF JOHN

- PARABLE
- ENRICHMENT PRESENTATION (SYNTHESIS)

THE MATERIAL

- LOCATION: PARABLE SHELVES
- PIECES: BASKET CONTAINING 40 GOLD PARABLE CARDS (RECTANGLES) AND 15 GOLD "I AM" CARDS (TRIANGLES); "GOSPEL OF JOHN" BOX FOR SORTING; BOX OF CONTEXT CARDS
- UNDERLAY: NONE

BACKGROUND

The "I Am" statements are those made by Jesus in the Gospel of John. In the previous lesson, Parable Synthesis 1 (pp. 132-138), children discovered the abundance of the parables. In that lesson the question of the triangle-shaped tiles will come up. This presentation is a response to that question.

NOTES ON THE MATERIAL

Find the material in a large basket placed on the lowest shelf of one of the parable shelves. Although you will focus only on the "I Am" statements, the material is a complete set of Jesus' parables (written on gold, wooden, rectangular cards) and a complete set of Jesus' "I Am" statements (written on gold, wooden, triangular cards). The cards are mixed together in a large basket in the classroom.

This presentation uses the fifteen "I Am" cards and a sorting box representing the Gospel of John. The "I Am" cards are placed in the box in sequence (as they appear in John), so they can be matched with the context cards. The children use the fifteen context cards to find out what was happening when a particular "I Am" statement was made. (The choice of "I Am" statements and stories is based on the work of Raymond Brown and other Johannine scholars.)

Make a set of fifteen context cards by printing the words provided below onto cardboard. Laminate the context cards so they can be wiped clean from time to time and so they withstand frequent use by the children. On the cards, include *only* the indented text, *not* the card numbers *nor* the citations *nor* the italicized "I am" statement itself; these are provided for your convenience *only*:

Card One: *"I am he, the one who is speaking to you" (John 4:26).*

This took place near the Samaritan city of Sychar at Jacob's well. After the disciples had gone into the city to buy food, a woman came to the well to draw water. She and Jesus talked about "living water" that he will give. They then discussed her five husbands and the person she was presently living with. ("I have no husband," she had said honestly.) The question about where one should worship had come up because it was a point of disagreement between the Jews and the Samaritans. Jesus told her that the hour was coming when people would worship God neither on the mountain in Samaria nor in the temple in Jerusalem. They would worship God in spirit and in truth.

The woman at the well said to him, *"'I know that Messiah is coming' (who is called Christ). 'When he comes, he will proclaim all things to us.' Jesus said to her, 'I am he, the one who is speaking to you'" (John 4:25-26).*

Card Two: *"It is I; do not be afraid" (John 6:20; see also Matthew 14:22–[27]32 and Mark 6:45–[50]52).*

In the evening the disciples got into a boat and started across the Sea of Galilee to Capernaum. Jesus was still on the mountain by himself, where he had withdrawn after the 5,000 moved to make him king after they had been fed by the five barley loaves and two fish. The wind was blowing, so the sea was rough.

"When they had rowed about three or four miles, they saw Jesus walking on the sea and coming near the boat, and they were terrified. But he said to them, 'It is I; do not be afraid'" (John 6:19-20).

Card Three: *"I am the bread of life" (John 6:35; see also John 6:48 and 6:51).*

The crowd followed Jesus and the disciples across the Sea of Galilee to Capernaum and found him there in the synagogue, teaching. He talked about "bread from heaven"; they thought he meant the manna that their ancestors ate in the wilderness. He then said, *"'For the bread of God is that which comes down from heaven and gives life to the world.' They said to him, 'Sir, give us this bread always.' Jesus said to them, 'I am the bread of life'" (John 6:33-35a).*

Jesus then goes on to say that those who come to him will never be hungry or thirsty.

During the discourse that follows, Jesus also says at John 6:48, *"I am the bread of life,"* and at 6:51, *"I am the living bread that came down from heaven."*

Card Four: *"I am the light of the world"* *(John 8:12; see also John 9:5 and 12:46).*

Jesus went in secret to the Festival of Booths in Jerusalem, but he sat down and began to teach in the temple one morning. The scribes and the Pharisees brought a woman who had been caught in adultery. The law of Moses commanded them to stone her to death. To test Jesus, they wanted to know what he would do. Jesus wrote with his finger on the ground. They kept questioning him. *"He straightened up and said, 'Let anyone among you who is without sin be the first to throw a stone at her.' He then bent down and wrote again on the ground. They went away, one by one, beginning with the elders" (John 8:7-9a).*

"'Woman, where are they? Has no one condemned you?' She said 'No one, sir.' And Jesus said, 'Neither do I condemn you. Go your way, and from now on do not sin again.' Again Jesus spoke to them, saying, 'I am the light of the world'" (John 8:10b-12a).

Jesus also spoke these words while he was teaching in the treasury of the temple. He also said, *"Whoever follows me will never walk in darkness but will have the light of life" (John 8:12b).* No one arrested him because his time had not yet come.

He continued to teach until they picked up stones (John 8:59). He left the temple and came upon a man blind from birth. At John 9:5 he said, *"As long as I am in the world, I am the light of the world."* He then spit on the ground and made mud to spread on the blind man's eyes. The man was told then to go wash in the pool of Siloam (which means Sent).

At John 12:46 he also said, *"I have come as the light of the world."*

Card Five: *"I am the one who gives testimony on my behalf"* *(John 8:18).*

During Jesus' discourse in the treasury, his testimony in John 8:12 was objected to by the Pharisees, because it was on his own behalf.

"In your law it is written that the testimony of two witnesses is valid. I testify on my own behalf, and the Father who sent me testifies on my behalf" (John 8:17-18).

Card Six: *"You are from below, I am from above; you are of this world, I am not of this world"* *(John 8:23).*

This discourse in the treasury continued. *"Again he said to them, 'I am going away, and you will search for me, but you will die in your sin. Where I am going,* you cannot come.' Then the Jews said, 'Is he going to kill himself? Is that what he means by saying, "Where I am going, you cannot come?"' He said to them, 'You are from below, I am from above, you are of this world'" (John 8:21-23).

Card Seven: *"Very truly, I tell you, before Abraham was, I am"* (John 8:58).

When Jesus began to talk about eternal life the crowd thought he was putting himself above Abraham and the prophets who died long ago. *"Jesus said to them, 'Very truly, I tell you, before Abraham was I am.' So they picked up stones to throw at him, but Jesus hid himself and went out of the temple"* (John 8:58-59).

Card Eight: *"You have seen him, and the one speaking with you is he"* (John 9:37).

After the discourse in the temple treasury, Jesus came upon the blind man and healed him. When people asked the man what happened, he told them that Jesus had healed him. The blind man began to be hounded by the Pharisees. They threatened him that if he continued to say that it was Jesus, rather than God, who healed him, he would be thrown out of the synagogue.

"Jesus heard that they had driven him out, and when he found him, he said, 'Do you believe in the Son of Man?' He answered, 'And who is he, sir? Tell me, so that I may believe in him.' Jesus said to him, 'You have seen him, and the one speaking with you is he'" (John 9:35-37).

Card Nine: *"I am the gate for the sheep"* (John 10:7–9).

It was winter and the time of the Festival of the Dedication (John 10:22). *"Jesus was walking in the temple in the portico of Solomon"* (John 10:23). *"The people asked him, 'How long will you keep us in suspense?'"* (John 10:24b). They wanted to know if he were really the messiah. He told them that he had already told them. He then began his discourse about sheep and shepherds which begins at John 10:1.

"So again Jesus said to them, 'Very truly, I tell you, I am the gate for the sheep'" (John 10:7).

Card Ten: *"I am the good shepherd"* (John 10:14; see also John 10:11).

"The hired hand runs away because a hired hand does not care for the sheep. I am the good shepherd" (John 10:13-14a).

The discourse about sheep and shepherds continued. The good shepherd will lay down his life for the sheep, and he knows his own, and they know him. At the end of the discourse, Jesus spoke about what his Father had given him and that "My Father and I are one."

The people were upset by Jesus' claim that "My Father and I are one" (John 10:31). They took up stones again to stone him for his blasphemy, *"...because you, though only a human being, are making yourself God"* (John 10:33).

"Jesus then went across the Jordan River, to the place John had been baptizing people earlier, and Jesus remained there" (John 10:40).

Card Eleven: *"I am the resurrection and the life"* (John 11:25–27).

Lazarus was ill in Bethany, "some two miles away" from Jerusalem. The sisters, Mary and Martha, sent Jesus a message, but Jesus stayed two days longer.

It was dangerous to go back to Judea. When Jesus and the disciples arrived in Bethany, Lazarus had already been in the tomb for four days. Many had come to Bethany from Jerusalem to console Mary and Martha. When Martha heard that Jesus was coming she went to meet him while Mary stayed at home.

"Jesus said to her, 'Your brother will rise again.' Martha said to him, 'I know that he will rise again in the resurrection on the last day.' Jesus said to her, 'I am the resurrection and the life'" (John 11:23-25a).

Martha sent word to Mary that Jesus was coming and he wanted to see her. Mary went out also to meet him. Mary said to him exactly what her sister had said to him, *"Lord, if you had been here, my brother would not have died"* (John 11:21 and 32).

A crowd was now gathering, because those who had come from Jerusalem had followed Mary. They all went to the tomb. The sisters and many in the crowd were weeping. Jesus too was greatly disturbed and wept.

Jesus was challenged by some from Jerusalem that he could heal the blind but not Lazarus. The stone was rolled back and the "stench" was great after four days. He called Lazarus out in a loud voice "for the sake of the crowd." The dead man came out.

This act prompted a council of the Pharisees. They were concerned that, if Jesus kept doing signs like this, everyone would believe in him. They were worried then that the Romans would come and destroy their holy place and nation. Caiaphas told them it was better for one to die than to lose the temple and the nation. From that day on they planned Jesus' death.

Card Twelve: *"I tell you this now, before it occurs, so that when it does occur, you may believe that I am he"* (John 13:19).

Jesus returned to the house of Lazarus six days before the Passover. He went from there into Jerusalem for the last time, sitting on the young donkey.

On Thursday that week Jesus and the disciples met in an upper room. During supper he washed the disciples' feet and told them that it was done to show that they ought to wash each other's feet, as if they were all servants to each other.

"'If you know these things, you are blessed if you do them. I am not speaking of all of you; I know whom I have chosen. But it is to fulfill the scripture, 'The one who ate my bread has lifted his heel against me. I tell you this now, before it occurs, so that when it does occur, you may believe that I am he'" (John 13:17-19).

He was very troubled and then told them, *"Very truly, I tell you, one of you will betray me" (John 13:21).* After Judas went out, Jesus gave them a new commandment: Love one another as I have loved you. He told them that where he was going they could not come. *"Just as I have loved you, you also should love one another. By this everyone will know that you are my disciples, if you have love for one another" (John 13:34–35).*

Peter vowed to lay down his life for Jesus, who tells him that before the cock crows Peter will have denied Jesus three times.

Card Thirteen: *"I am the way, and the truth, and the life" (John 14:5).*

Chapter 14 begins with Jesus comforting the disciples. *"Do not let your hearts be troubled" (John 14:1a).*

"Thomas said to him, 'Lord, we do not know where you are going. How can we know the way?' Jesus said to him, 'I am the way, and the truth, and the life'" (John 14:5-6a).

Card Fourteen: *"I am the true vine, and my Father is the vinegrower" (John 15:1).*

Jesus' discourse about the true vine is John 15:1–11. It begins abruptly with his words: *"I am the true vine, and my Father is the vinegrower."*

The theme is "… abide in my love." The ending is: *"I have said these things to you so that my joy may be in you, and that your joy may be complete" (John 15:11).* He then says (John 15:12–13): *"This is my commandment that you love another as I have loved you. No one has greater love than this, to lay down one's life for one's friends."* This affirmed the announcement of the new commandment made just after Judas left (John 13:34–35).

Jesus continued to comfort the disciples and to prepare them. He finally said the paradoxical: "I am going away, and I am coming to you." The "ruler of the world" is coming for him, but has no power over him, because he does as the Father commands him to do. Jesus then told them that even though he was going away, he would send the Advocate, the Holy Spirit to them.

Card Fifteen: *"I am he" (John 18:5).*

"Then Jesus, knowing all that was to happen to him, came forward and asked them, 'Whom are you looking for?' They answered, 'Jesus of Nazareth.' Jesus replied, 'I am he.' Judas, who betrayed him, was standing with them. When Jesus said to them, 'I am he,' they stepped back and fell to the ground" (John 18:4-6).

He asked them again who they were looking for and then told them to let the rest go. After Jesus told Peter to put away his sword, Jesus was taken away peacefully.

SPECIAL NOTES

Tip: The parable synthesis lessons (pp. 132-152) shift from the teaching objects for the six guiding parables to the more abstract and text-linked cards. This material is for children about nine years old and older. Children need to be comfortable with reading to enjoy working with the parables as texts.

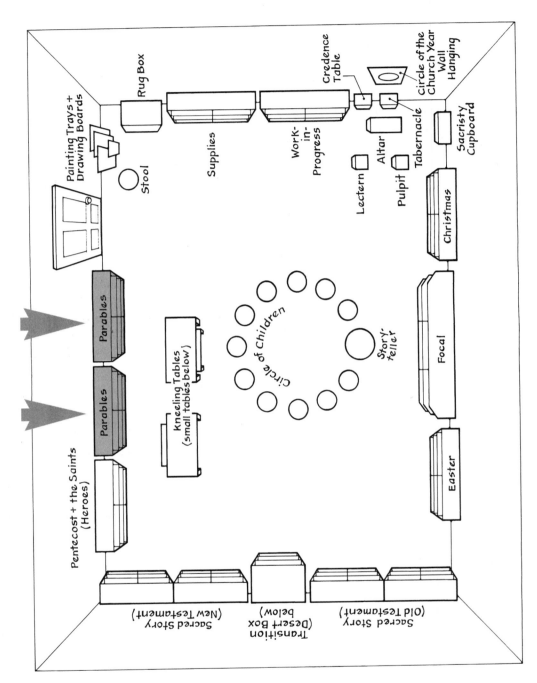

WHERE TO FIND MATERIALS

MOVEMENTS

Go to the shelf and bring the basket containing the parable cards and the "I Am" cards, along with the Gospel of John box and the box of context cards.

Separate the "I Am" statements (the triangles) from the parable cards (the rectangles). Put the "I Am" statements into their sorting box (the John box).

Hold each of the triangles with respect and curiosity as you read what is written on it. (As you work through the cards, sort them—in the John box—in sequence, according to the order they appear in the Gospel of John.)

Continue until the wondering begins to wane. Then place the box with the context cards in front of you.

Read the first context card. Place it in front of you in the middle of the circle. Repeat until all of the context cards and "I Am" statements are matched.

Place all of the context cards back in the box. As you place each card back, remember the story.

Place all of the "I Am" cards in the large basket with the parables. Return all materials to their shelves.

WORDS

Look at all of these. There are so many. Some of these are parables, but I wonder what these triangles could be? Let's sort them into this box and put the parables to the side. Then let's look carefully at each triangle.

"I am he, the one who is speaking to you." These are strange sayings.

I wonder what the speaker is trying to say?

I wonder why he talks about himself that way?

I wonder what happens when you add up all of these sayings?

These are the context cards.

Now, I wonder which "I Am" saying Jesus used then?

I wonder if we can tell John's story of Jesus with just the "I Am" sayings and their context? What is left out? Would you like to read the whole story to see? You can make that your work, if you like.

ENRICHMENT LESSON

PARABLE SYNTHESIS 3
THE PARABLE GAMES

LESSON NOTES

FOCUS: FEATURES OF THE PARABLES TOGETHER

- ● PARABLE
- ● ENRICHMENT PRESENTATION (SYNTHESIS)

THE MATERIAL

- ● LOCATION: PARABLE SHELVES
- ● PIECES: BASKET CONTAINING 40 GOLD PARABLE CARDS (RECTANGLES) AND 23 YELLOW PARABLE GAME CARDS (ALSO RECTANGLES)
- ● UNDERLAY: NONE

BACKGROUND

The parable games are third-level abstractions. First-level sensorial awareness results from deep play with particular parables (pp. 77-131). The second level of abstraction is discovered by laying out and using all the parable cards (pp. 132-147). The third level of abstraction is found by playing games to discover some of the features of the whole group, or corpus, of parables. These games are the focus of this session.

NOTES ON THE MATERIAL

These game cards are used together with the parable cards used in Parable Synthesis 1—All the Parables (pp. 132-138). The text used on the parable cards is the *New Revised Standard Version*. There are thirty-one different parables excluding doubles and triples. There are forty parables when doubles and triples are included. There are twelve triples, eight doubles and twenty singles, for a total of forty cards. (Text from Luke appears on twenty cards, from Matthew on fourteen and from Mark on six.) When we consider parables unique to each synoptic gospel, we find that Luke has the most and Mark the least. (Luke has eleven unique ones, Matthew has seven, and Mark has one.)

The wooden game cards are yellow to remind children of the gold parable boxes. The cards are rectangles about 5" x 7½". If you make the cards yourself, you could use foamcore, but wood gives the cards more strength and invites the children's respect.

If you use foamcore that is yellow only on one side, glue yellow paper with the text printed on it on the other side. You can then color the edges of the Foamcore with a yellow felt marker.

Find the cards in a basket on the lowest shelf of one of the parable shelves. Stand the cards up so the children can see what is written on the first card, with the remaining cards standing in a line behind it, one behind the other. In this way each card is "shouting out" to be picked up so the particular game can begin.

The text of the first card is centered and spread out, as shown here:

```
┌─────────────────────────────┐
│       Parable Games         │
│          BEWARE             │
│         Parables            │
│            can              │
│          turn you           │
│        upside down          │
│            and              │
│         inside out.         │
└─────────────────────────────┘
```

The text of the game cards follows. Do *not* include the italicized answers on the cards. Children discover these answers by using the game cards to play with the parable cards. (See Parable Synthesis 1—All the Parables, pp. 132-138 for a description of the parable cards.)

1. Come play this game: What is the longest parable? *A Man Had Two Sons*

2. Come play this game: What are the three longest parables? *A Man Had Two Sons; A Man Going On a Journey; A King Who Wished to Settle Accounts*

3. Come play this game: What is the shortest parable? *The Net (twenty-one words)*

4. Come play this game: Find the parables in more than one gospel. Do they say the same when they are in a different gospel? *There are ten. Sometimes they do.*

5. Come play this game: How many parables are in the Gospel of John? *None*

6. Come play this game: What parables are in only one gospel? *See the list on pages 133-134.*

7. Come play this game: How many parables are in the Gospel of Matthew? *Seventeen*

8. Come play this game: What gospel has the most parables? *Luke—there are twenty-two.*

9. Come play this game: What gospel has the fewest parables? *Mark—there are six.*

10. Come play this game: Find the parables that are in only two gospels. *See the list on pages 133-134.*

11. Come play this game: What parables are in three gospels? *See the list on pages 133-134.*

12. Come play this game: What parables are in four gospels? *None*

13. Come play this game: What parable is the most confusing for you? Why?

14. Come play this game: What parable is the most clear? Why?

15. Come play this game: What parable do you like best? Why?

16. Come play this game: What parable is the least important one? Why?

17. Come play this game: What parable do you like least? Why?

18. Come play this game: What parable is the most important one? Why?

19. Come play this game: Name the parables! Name your favorite. Name the shortest. Name the longest. Name the funniest. Name the saddest. Name the happiest. Name them all!

20. Come play this game: Make up your own parable. One good parable deserves another. Can you make up one that is right for you?

21. Come play this game: What shape do the parables make when you put them all together?

22. Come play this game: Create a parable box presentation and materials for your favorite parable.

SPECIAL NOTES

Tip: The Parable Synthesis lessons (All the Parables, The "I Am" Statements and The Parable Games, pp. 132-152) shift from the teaching objects for the six guiding parables to the more abstract and text-linked cards. This material is for children about nine years old and older. Children need to be comfortable with reading to enjoy working with the parables as texts.

When you invite the children to work, one option offered is doing "side-by-sides." This refers to the practice of putting two stories—or, in this case, two parable cards—next to each other to make discoveries about how two stories talk to each other.

MOVEMENTS

You do not need a rug for this lesson. There are too many parable cards to fit on a single rug.

Go to the parable shelf and bring the basket of parable cards and parable games to the circle. Place it beside you.

Lean forward or get on your knees and slowly and carefully spread out the parable cards in a large rectangle of eight cards by five cards. Leave the "I Am" statements in the basket for this lesson.

Lean back. Enjoy the abundance of parables.

Pause. Move your hand over the multitude of parables.

Pause for a moment because you are getting ready to introduce the parable games. Place the parable games beside the parable cards.

Take out the title card and point to what it says. Read it.

Pick up the second card, with Question #1. Read it and show how it invites the children to play.

WORDS

We have been given a gift. It was given to us even before we were born. It is a gift from Jesus himself. It is the parables.

Here are all of the parables in the Bible written on cards.

Here are the parable games.

When the parable games invite you to come and play, they ask you many questions. There is no way to find out the answers except by asking the parables, so the parables play, too. They have asked you many questions, now you can ask them questions. Let's see how this works.

You really do need to be careful. Parables can confuse you into finding out things you don't even have questions for yet.

Let's see now. It says, "What is the longest parable?" That's easy. Let's look at all the cards with long parables on them and find the longest. See? I am dividing the whole group into short, middle and long. Look. Here are the longest of the long.

There. That is the longest. Be careful. Sometimes you have to count every word.

Now it is your turn. Perhaps you would like to make this your work today. There are many more game cards inviting you to come play if you are ready.

MOVEMENTS

If you have been working with a child individually you can end here. If you have made this a group presentation you will need to pause now and look around the circle. Speak slowly and with feeling.

WORDS

There are many things in this room that you can make your work today. You may even have unfinished work you would like to finish. Making your own lesson about someone special to you is very good work too, if you would like to choose it.

Dismiss the children one by one to go get out their work after it has been carefully chosen.

Now, what work would you like to get out today?